—African-American Biographies—

JACKIE ROBINSON

Baseball's Civil Rights Legend

Series Consultant:
Dr. Russell L. Adams, Chairman
Department of Afro-American Studies, Howard University

Karen Mueller Coombs

Enslow Publishers, Inc.
44 Fadem Road   PO Box 38
Box 699   Aldershot
Springfield, NJ 07081   Hants GU12 6BP
USA   UK

To Bill, who stood at many crossroads of
his own—and took the right fork.

To Lisa, because I love her.

And especially to Jon—for surviving.

Library of Congress Cataloging-in-Publication Data

Coombs, Karen Mueller, 1947–
    Jackie Robinson: baseball's civil rights legend / Karen Mueller Coombs.
        p. cm.—(African-American biographies)
    Includes bibliographical references and index.
    Summary: Explores the life and career of Jackie Robinson, from his
childhood in Pasadena, California, through his struggles with prejudice
and discrimination, to his success as a major league baseball player.
    ISBN 0-89490-690-9
    1. Robinson, Jackie, 1919-1972—Juvenile literature. 2. Afro-American
baseball players—Biography—Juvenile literature. 3. Brooklyn Dodgers
(Baseball team)—History—Juvenile literature.
    [1. Robinson, Jackie, 1919-1972. 2. Baseball players.
3. Afro-Americans—Biography.] I. Title. II. Series.
GV865.R6C66   1997
796.357'092—dc20
[B]
                                                    96-20584
                                                       CIP
                                                        AC
Printed in the U.S.A.

10 9 8 7 6 5 4 3 2 1

Illustration Credits:
AP/Wide World Photos, pp. 99, 101; Brooklyn Public Library, Brooklyn
Collection, pp. 66, 76; Library of Congress, p. 33; National Baseball
Library and Archive, Cooperstown, New York, pp. 61, 68, 105, 109;
Pasadena City College, pp. 18, 21; University of California at Los
Angeles Photo Department, p. 23; UPI/Bettmann, pp. 28, 39, 59, 63, 74,
91, 93, 103. .

Cover Illustration:
FPG International

Contents

NOTE TO READER

In the days when Jackie Robinson was breaking the color barrier in modern major league baseball, some people felt free to use words and names that are not acceptable today. This book contains some of those words. They are included because they help show what obstacles Robinson had to overcome, and how strong he had to be to battle the racial prejudice against African Americans in baseball—and in American society.

1

AT THE
CROSSROADS

hey're waiting for you in the jungles, black boy!"

"We don't want you here, nigger."[1]

Twenty-eight-year-old Jackie Robinson stepped up to bat for the Brooklyn Dodgers one April day in 1947. Ignoring the hateful words spewing at him from the visitors' dugout, he took his stance at the plate. With his bat in its usual position—cocked high over his shoulder—he waited for the first pitch.

When he signed to become the twentieth century's first African American to play major league baseball, Robinson had been warned to expect brutal treatment from fans and players. Although he *had* expected it, especially from people from the Deep South, the team now slinging curses was the Philadelphia Phillies.

By 1947 African-American men had fought and died for the United States in two world wars. Many people, however, such as Phillies' team manager Ben Chapman, still believed that African Americans did not belong in major league baseball. Chapman, from Alabama, had ordered his players to taunt Robinson. If Robinson fought back, the act might cause a race riot, proving that blacks and whites should not play in the same league.

African Americans had not always been excluded from professional baseball. During the 1870s, 1880s, and 1890s, more than sixty blacks played with whites on professional teams. As segregation emerged as an American custom, baseball's color barrier appeared. In 1887 white players began refusing to play against teams with black players. Some white players even refused to have their picture taken with their own black teammates. By 1892 African Americans were no longer welcome in organized baseball. So they formed their own separate leagues. Now, in 1947, Jackie Robinson was battering at the barrier that separated African Americans from the national pastime.

While bench jockeying—rival players yelling nasty remarks from their dugout—has always been part of baseball, the jeers spouting from the Phillies' bench were worse than anyone had ever heard. Even in Robinson's first four games as a Dodger, the taunts had not been as cruel.

The Phillies made nasty comments about Robinson's looks. They warned his fellow Dodgers they would get sores and diseases if they touched Robinson's comb or towel. "At no time in my life have I heard racial venom and dugout abuse to match the abuse . . . sprayed on Robinson that night," wrote Brooklyn's traveling secretary Harold Parrott.[2]

Robinson seemed calm, but he was not playing as well as he could. He was, after all, a human being, a man who always stood up for himself when someone offended his dignity. This was only his fifth game as a Dodger. How much longer could he turn the other cheek? He must have been crazy, he told himself, to think that his ball-playing skills would win over people so full of racial prejudice and hatred.[3]

Years later Robinson wrote that he briefly thought how wonderful it would feel to walk over to the Phillies' dugout, grab one of his white tormentors, and punch in the lout's teeth. Robinson knew that would mean the end of his baseball career. It would also ruin the chances of other African-American players hoping to move into the major leagues. Still he was tempted.[4]

If only his teammates would back him up the way they did other Dodgers being unfairly badgered. Many of the Brooklyn players themselves, however, did not want an African American in the league. So there was little hope of support from other Dodgers if Robinson fought back.

Jackie Robinson was at a crossroads. Would he hold fast and endure the insults, opening the way for others of his race—and changing sports history? Or would he stand up to his abusers and defend himself against the slurs to his dignity as a human being?

He thought of Branch Rickey, the general manager of the Dodgers, who had picked Robinson to become the first African American in the National League. Rickey had been at a crossroads too. His family and trusted advisers worried that the sixty-three-year-old man's health and reputation would suffer if he tried to integrate baseball. They urged him not to be the one to break tradition. Still, Rickey had taken on the challenge. He had brought Jackie Robinson into the big leagues.

Robinson later wrote, ". . . this day of all the unpleasant days in my life, brought me nearer to cracking up than I ever had been."[5] Now, listening to the ugly taunts and catcalls, Robinson made his decision. He would honor Rickey's trust and continue to blaze a trail for African Americans. Robinson turned his mind back to baseball—and in the eighth inning crossed home plate for the game's only run.

The heckling continued during the next two games. Then an unexpected event happened. Eddie

Stanky, the Dodger second baseman, and like Ben Chapman, from the South, faced the Phillies' dugout. "Listen, you yellow-bellied cowards," he shouted, "Why don't you yell at somebody who can answer back?"[6] Other Dodgers also leaped to Robinson's defense.

Rickey had told Robinson that if he could win the team's respect and get the players to stand behind him, the bid to integrate baseball would succeed. Now the Phillies' obnoxious behavior' had forced the Dodgers to unite. Chapman's plan had backfired. Instead of forcing Robinson into a rage, the Phillies had made him a real member of the Dodgers. Baseball's "noble experiment," its attempt to integrate the national pastime, seemed headed for success.

2

THE KID FROM PEPPER STREET

igger! Nigger! Nigger!" the little girl yelled across Pepper Street at eight-year-old Jackie Robinson.

The boy would not put up with that kind of treatment. His mother, Mallie Robinson, had taught him to respect himself and to demand respect from others.

"You're nothing but a cracker!" he shouted back. His older brother Edgar had told Jackie that this was the worst insult he could give a white person.

"Soda cracker's good to eat. Nigger's only good to beat," jeered the girl.[1]

Many such clashes occurred in Jackie's young life.

Sometimes stones flew back and forth along with the taunts. Once someone burned a cross on the family's front lawn. At least here—in Pasadena, California— Jackie *could* fight back, unlike the place where he had been born.

Jack Roosevelt Robinson, the grandson of a slave, was born in a cabin in Cairo, Georgia, on January 31, 1919. He was the youngest child of Jerry and Mallie Robinson, joining siblings Edgar, Frank, Mack, and Willa Mae.

The Robinsons sharecropped for the Sassers, a white family. In exchange for raising corn, potatoes, and sugar cane for Mr. Sasser, the Robinsons received from him a place to live and coupons called chits. These chits could be exchanged for provisions at the Sassers' store. Using chits made it impossible to earn and save money. So, even at its best, sharecropping was a hard way to earn a living.

When Jackie was six months old his father left the family. Determined to give her children a good life, Robinson's mother, Mallie, decided to leave Georgia. The Ku Klux Klan, a white supremacy group, operated in the state. Mallie felt that there was little opportunity for African-American children living where the Klan used fear, force, and murder to ensure that Jim Crow laws were honored and obeyed.

Jim Crow was the name given to laws in the South that allowed people to treat blacks differently from whites. These laws meant that blacks and whites could not attend the same schools, sleep in the same hotels, eat in the same restaurants, be healed in the same hospitals, wait in the same waiting rooms, or ride in the same train cars. Jim Crow meant separate drinking fountains, toilets, ticket windows—even exits and entrances—for blacks and whites. In some areas of the South it was even against the law for blacks and whites to play a game of checkers together.

In the spring of 1920 Mallie Robinson packed her family's few belongings into straw suitcases. She and her five children—ages ten, nine, five, two, and fourteen months—rode a train west to Pasadena, California, near Los Angeles. They moved in with relatives.

Pasadena was a lovely town of elegant houses and streets. Flowering shrubs, eucalyptus, and orange blossoms perfumed the air. Even here, however, blacks lived isolated from whites; renting or buying homes in certain areas of town, swimming in the public pool only on Tuesdays, sitting in separate sections in movie theaters, and working at menial jobs. The only work that Mallie Robinson could find was as a housekeeper.

Mallie Robinson's hard work and meager wages barely kept the family going. Some accounts say that the Robinsons sometimes went on welfare. According to Jackie's sister, Willa Mae, however, the family never accepted welfare.[2]

Finally, when Jackie was about four, his family rented, and eventually bought, a house at 121 Pepper

Street in a modest area of town occupied only by whites. Here, the youngest Robinson learned to stand up for himself against hostile white neighbors. Some neighbors even started a petition, hoping to drive the Robinsons out of the area. The family's next-door neighbor, remembering the favors Jackie's older brother Edgar had done for her, refused to sign. The petition failed.

A proud religious woman, Mallie Robinson encouraged her children to be helpful to the neighbors. She also expected the children to do well in school, to attend church, and to share what little they had. Some meals were only bread soaked in milk and sugar. The bread and milk were often unsold extras given to the family by the baker and the local milk carrier.

Mallie Robinson's work took her away from her family for most of the day. She demanded that her children act responsibly while looking out for themselves and for each other. When Willa Mae, Jackie's older sister and babysitter, started school, Jackie went with her. He played in the sandbox while his sister watched him from inside her classroom.

The schoolchildren soon learned that Jackie was good at sports. They began offering him food and dimes to play on their teams at recess. Even at that young age, Jackie's talents were obvious.

When Jackie started school at Cleveland Elementary he was not very interested in academics.

He was better than everyone else at sports though. Marbles, soccer, handball, dodgeball, table tennis, and tennis—he excelled at every sport.

Jackie came by his talent naturally. All his older siblings were fine athletes. Willa Mae shone in all the sports open to women, including basketball, track, and soccer. In 1936 Jack's brother Mack won a silver medal when he placed second in the 200-meter dash in the Olympic Games held in Berlin, Germany. Unfortunately for the Robinsons, the winner—an African American named Jesse Owens—got all the attention.

By the time he attended Washington Junior High, Robinson was a leader in the sports arena. He would study his opponents, plan a strategy—then win. This showed the intelligence that eventually made him one of the most valuable players on the baseball diamond, a player for whom personal glory was not as important as the game and the team.

When Robinson competed for his school teams— first Washington Junior High and later John Muir Technical High—opposing players tried to anger Robinson. They thought that he would lose his concentration and play poorly. The strategy did not work. Robinson was interested only in winning, nothing else. The more angry he felt, the better he played.

Though busy with sports—and with homework, chores, and Sunday school—Robinson still had plenty of free time during his junior and senior high school years. Some of that time he filled by earning money: servicing a paper route, cutting grass, running errands, shining shoes, and selling hot dogs at sporting events. Some of that time, though, he filled with mischief.

The neighborhood was now racially mixed. Robinson, along with other teenaged boys who loved sports, formed the Pepper Street Gang. The gang was nothing like the gangs of today. Members included blacks, whites, Asians, and Hispanics. Sports took up most of the gang's time. The members also got into minor scrapes with the law though. Their troublemaking included hurling rocks or dirt at passing cars, knocking out street lights, stealing food, smashing windows, raiding orchards, and snatching golf balls from the local course and selling them back to the golfers.

Robinson had more nerve than the others and paid less attention to authority. So he usually found the trouble first. Although there was no Jim Crow law against blacks and whites eating in the same restaurant, waitresses and waiters often refused to serve African Americans. Robinson insisted that the gang members shake up the local Woolworth's by sitting at the lunch counter until they got waited on—no matter how long it took. Once he coaxed the gang to swim in the drinking water reservoir. For this prank the police hauled the boys to jail—all sixteen teenagers crowded into one cell. When one of the African Americans complained of thirst, the sheriff said, "The coon's hungry. Go buy a watermelon."[3] Racists make unkind jokes about African Americans' supposed fondness for watermelon, so this comment was intended as ridicule.

Fortunately, Robinson's misdeeds never took him any farther than the local police station. Mallie Robinson's strong influence likely kept her son out of serious trouble. Robinson called her a courageous woman, who gave him the basic values to live a life of honor.[4] Local mechanic Carl Anderson took notice of the fatherless boy. Anderson warned Robinson against running with a pack and urged him to march to his own drum.

Karl Downs, pastor of the family's church, also built a relationship with the teenaged Robinson that lasted for many years. Because of Reverend Downs's influence, the boy helped build a youth center in the church and taught Sunday school.

Sports, however, gave direction to Robinson's life. He saw sports as a way to escape poverty, said a childhood friend.[5] At John Muir Technical High School, Robinson won letters in basketball, football, baseball, and track. He played so well that opposing coaches told their teams that if they could stop Robinson they could win the game.

Had Jackie Robinson been white, major universities would have lined up with offers of scholarships for the talented young senior. By his 1937 graduation, however, no such offers had appeared.

3

FOUR-LETTER
ATHLETE

 n the autumn of 1937 Robinson enrolled at
Pasadena Junior College. Again he became a
powerhouse on the field, the court, the track,
and the diamond. Racial incidents nevertheless marred
his college experience. At one of his first football
practices, some white Oklahoma teammates—recruited
to Pasadena by the coach—were unhappy about playing
with blacks. They created such hostility that the coach
canceled practice. Working together, the coach,
Robinson, and other African-American players on the
team finally achieved peace with the Oklahomans.

In 1937, Jackie Robinson enrolled at Pasadena Junior College, and became a sensation on the track, as well as other sports.

One incident may or may not have been related to Robinson's race. At the very least it showed a lack of concern for the young athlete. Early in the season Robinson twisted his ankle and left the gridiron limping. An immediate X-ray should have been in order, but the trainer merely bandaged the ankle. A few days later, severe pain sent Robinson to the emergency room. X-rays showed a broken bone. The break did not require a cast, but walking and playing on the ankle had made the injury worse. Robinson's ankle bothered him for the rest of his life.

Another time the football team traveled to Phoenix, Arizona. Upon checking into the hotel, the black players learned that they could not stay there, but were to be housed in a separate hotel. This made Robinson and the other African Americans so angry that they refused the rooms given to them.[1] Instead they sat up in the lobby all night. It was a public rejection that Jackie Robinson was to undergo many times in the future, even after he became famous.

In contrast to this insulting treatment, Robinson and two other athletes became the first African Americans named to the student honor society at the college. They used the prestige of this position to try to end the segregated seating of the Civic Auditorium, where students went for concerts and movies. Though there were no laws requiring separate seating, blacks always sat in the balcony. Robinson prodded them to leave the balcony and join the white students on the main floor. Hesitant to challenge tradition, the blacks ignored his pleas.

He was not as easily ignored on the playing field, though, propelling Pasadena's teams to championships in baseball, football, and basketball. In basketball Robinson was the top scorer on the team and the best player in the conference. He continued to excel in track and field. One May day in 1938 particularly stood out. At a track meet in Pomona, California, Robinson asked to take his broad jumps before the start of competition. On his third jump he flew twenty-five feet, six-and-a-half inches, winning the event— and breaking the record set by his brother Mack.

Then he hurried into a waiting car. Changing clothes on the way, he was driven to Glendale, forty miles away. There, a couple of hits and a stolen base by Robinson helped power his baseball team to the league championship.

Other teams still singled him out as the player to stop. Since Robinson never looked for a fight, but never walked away from one either, these tactics sometimes led to conflict during games.[2]

Once a basketball opponent from Long Beach State kept poking his fingers in Robinson's face, even in his mouth. The next time the finger came his way, Robinson bit it—hard. A near riot ensued. The two

Jackie Robinson proved himself a talented basketball player while at Pasadena Junior College.

schools canceled all future competition between them.

Robinson, now twenty, graduated from Pasadena Junior College in the spring of 1939. Called the greatest all-around athlete in California sports, he had earned such nicknames as the "Dusky Flash," "Midnight Express," and "The Dark Demon." Major universities that had ignored him two years earlier now eagerly courted him. He was leaning toward a scholarship to UCLA when a family tragedy helped him decide. Jackie's brother Frank died in a motorcycle accident. Attending UCLA meant that Robinson would be nearby to help his mother as well as Frank's widow and two young children.

Being on scholarship did not mean that Robinson had it easy. He was always short of money. Although the Robinson family had the first telephone on the block and owned a car by the middle of the 1930s, lack of money for food and basics was often a problem. During football and basketball season, the school offered meals to the players. Track and baseball did not offer such a training table. Robinson had less enthusiasm for college baseball and less success in it than in football and basketball, perhaps because he did not eat as well during baseball season.

Part-time jobs helped Robinson's money problems. He once worked as a valet and a busboy at Warner Brothers movie studio. A friend also helped him earn

At the University of California in Los Angeles, Robinson made history by becoming the school's first athlete to letter in four sports—football, basketball, baseball, and track and field.

money by scalping the football tickets that Robinson received as a member of the team.[3]

Again there were "incidents." One day in his first months at UCLA, a white motorist yelled racial insults at Robinson and some friends. Robinson answered back. The street argument nearly turned into a race riot when police arrived. Surrounded by a crowd of African Americans, one police officer began reaching for his gun. Changing his mind, he simply arrested Robinson.

Charging him with suspicion of robbery, resisting arrest, and blocking a street, the police jailed Robinson for the night. They released him on bond the next morning. Though the more serious charges were dropped, the charge of blocking a street became part of Robinson's record.

His night in jail did not hurt Robinson's chances to shine as an all-star player. He made history by becoming UCLA's first four-letter man—in football, basketball, baseball, and track. The publicity that his brush with the law received might have made Robinson wary, however, because he made few close friends on campus. Robinson seemed withdrawn and unfriendly, said the late professional football player and movie actor Woody Strode, a senior on the UCLA football team the year that Robinson joined. Even on the field he kept to himself.[4]

One person made Robinson feel at ease, however.

Rachel Isum was a freshman in 1940, the year that she met Robinson. "She became the most important and helpful and encouraging person I ever met in my whole life," Robinson said. "When I became bitter or discouraged, she was always there with the help I needed."[5]

By early 1941 Robinson was fed up with being too broke to help support his mother or even to entertain Rachel. He knew that he wanted to make his living in sports, probably physical education or coaching, and believed that a college degree did not help an African-American get a job. Robinson, now twenty-two, quit school only a few months before graduation.

Today managers of professional sports teams would beg to sign a player of such superb achievements and talent. In 1941, though, professional sports were closed to African-American athletes and offered Robinson no shining hope for his future.

4

FIGHTING

UNCLE SAM

fter leaving UCLA in 1941, Robinson worked briefly at a camp in Atascadero, California, sponsored by the National Youth Administration. There, he played shortstop on the camp baseball team and worked with disadvantaged children. Later he combined semiprofessional football and part-time construction work in Hawaii.

When the Hawaiian football season ended, Robinson decided to go home. He and Rachel had been exchanging letters, and he was eager to continue their relationship. He sailed for the mainland on

December 5, 1941, and was at sea when Japan bombed Pearl Harbor two days later.

In March 1942 Robinson worked out with baseball's Chicago White Sox, who were training in Pasadena. The manager admitted that Robinson played well enough to be worth $50,000 to any professional club. Yet he made him no offer. Robinson could not have accepted an offer anyway. The day before, he had been drafted into the Army.

Robinson did three months of basic training at Fort Riley, Kansas, where Joe Louis, the heavyweight boxing champion, was also briefly stationed.[1] Soon after, Robinson applied for Officer Candidate School (OCS), which trained qualified soldiers to become officers. OCS at Fort Riley ignored his application.

When Robinson announced OCS had not accepted him, Joe Louis made a phone call to Truman Gibson, an African American working as special assistant to the secretary of war. A short time later OCS approved Robinson's application.

In January 1943 Jackie Robinson was commissioned as a second lieutenant. His new assignment was morale officer to a unit of African-American soldiers. At that time military units were not integrated. Black soldiers worked, ate, and slept apart from white soldiers. As morale officer, Robinson made certain his men were treated as well as other soldiers on base.

Although he never fought in World War II, while in the Army Robinson did what he could to battle discrimination against African Americans in the military.

A few of his experiences probably had Robinson wishing for his own morale booster. His relationship with Rachel was on-again, off-again. When he went out for the Fort Riley baseball team, the coach told him he could not play for them, but would instead have to join the "colored" team. No such team existed.

Although they did not know Robinson at the time, Pete Reiser and Dixie Walker—soldiers who later became Robinson's teammates on the Brooklyn Dodgers—were present that day. After the baseball coach told his "joke" about the fictional black team, Robinson said nothing, according to Reiser. He simply stood for a while, watching the team work out, then turned and walked away by himself. Years later Reiser still remembered that lonely exit.[2]

The Fort Riley football coach begged Robinson to join his team, but after learning that he would have to sit out any games played against southern teams, Robinson refused.

These experiences probably made Robinson more determined to be an effective morale officer for his men. It was not an easy job. White soldiers on base had the best of everything, even in the canteen, where off-duty soldiers went for food and entertainment. The canteen had plenty of tables and stools reserved for whites, but only a few for blacks.

Robinson telephoned a superior officer to complain of this unfair treatment. Not knowing

Robinson was African American, the major asked how Robinson would like to have his wife sitting next to a "nigger." Robinson flew into a rage, yelling at the major loud enough that anyone within earshot of Robinson's office could hear.[3]

Robinson got more seats for his men. Shortly after, he also got transferred to an African-American tank battalion at Fort Hood, Texas, where he became a platoon leader. Robinson knew little about tanks and confessed this to his men. They respected his honesty and performed well for him, earning Robinson praise from his commanding officer Colonel Paul Bates.

Colonel Bates's high opinion of Robinson proved useful in August 1944, when Bates was called to testify for Robinson in court. A month earlier Robinson had sat down near the middle of a bus with a woman he knew, a light-skinned African American. In Texas, buses were legally segregated; whites sat near the front, blacks were sent to the back.

The bus driver ordered Robinson, but not his seatmate, to move to the back of the bus. Knowing that the Army was banning segregated seating on bases, he refused. The driver stopped the bus and insisted. Angry words flew among the driver, the white passengers, and Robinson. When the bus finally arrived at the depot, military police detained Robinson and later charged him with insubordination.

Colonel Bates refused to sign the papers allowing

a court-martial. The Army moved Robinson to another unit, whose commander did sign them. After the colonel and other members of Robinson's battalion testified as to his character and reputation, however, the lieutenant was cleared of all charges.

Nevertheless Robinson's Army life was over. The military now viewed Robinson as a troublemaker. After a few more transfers, the Army honorably discharged him in November 1944, claiming his old ankle injury made him unfit for active duty. This disability had not stopped the Army from drafting Jackie Robinson. Now it became the Army's excuse for getting rid of him.

Relieved to be out of the military, Robinson patched up his relationship with Rachel and gave her an engagement ring before she left for a nursing job in New York. He also began job hunting. He applied for coaching positions at a number of colleges. A few even made him offers—until they learned that he was not white.[4]

Robinson spent that winter of 1944–1945 coaching men's basketball at Sam Houston College, a tiny African-American college in Texas. He also wrote a letter to the Kansas City Monarchs, the top professional baseball team in the Negro Leagues. He asked for a job. In the spring of 1945 Robinson reported for a tryout. The Monarchs hired him to play shortstop for $100 a week, minus meals and expenses.

Robinson's new job seemed a mixed blessing. He found it offensive that there even were separate leagues for black players. They should be playing in the majors with the white players. Fellow Monarch Othello Renfroe said that Robinson constantly told his teammates to be ready. Soon, he predicted, major league baseball would sign one of them.[5]

Robinson's background, experiences, and beliefs were different from many of his teammates'. Robinson was one of the few Monarchs who had a college education. A young man who set high standards for himself, Robinson did not take part in the drinking, partying, and smoking that some of the other players fancied. He did not enjoy the practical jokes and the horseplay among teammates. Mostly he disliked the lifestyle Negro Leaguers endured, even that of the Monarchs—the most famous team in the league. Robinson claimed that it was "a pretty miserable way to make a buck."[6]

Negro League teams traveled from town to town, mostly throughout the East and South. Battered buses or cars often carried them through the night to the next day's game. Sometimes the team played four games a day in two different towns, often on diamonds that were merely sandlots or farm fields. If the players were lucky enough to stop for the night, they had a hard time finding a hotel that would accept African Americans. The players often slept on the bus,

When Robinson traveled throughout the South with the Kansas City Monarchs, he encountered Jim Crow laws, which made it difficult for African Americans to find places to eat and sleep. At this restaurant, a separate dining area for African-American customers was located behind the toilets.

sometimes even on the floor of a railroad station. Few restaurants on the road allowed African Americans to enter. The men's meals were often takeout bought at the back door of the restaurant or food bought at grocery stores, then eaten on the bus. At gas stations, African Americans were forbidden to use the restrooms.

The proud Robinson would not tolerate this treatment. One time, when told that he could not use the restroom, Robinson ordered the attendant to stop putting gas into the bus. If the man did not let the players use the restroom, they would not buy a hundred gallons of gas from him. The players were allowed to use the restroom.

Another time Robinson punched a station attendant who cursed him when he used the restroom. In that part of the country, that act could have gotten him lynched.

Robinson's efforts changed the way the team thought and behaved. From then on, at any gas stop, the team first asked if they could use the restroom. If they could not, they did not buy gas.

As demeaning and demanding as life with the Monarchs was, Robinson still played well. No one kept official statistics, but researchers estimate that he batted .387 for the season. This means that he hit safely nearly 40 percent of the time. Any batting average above .300 is considered outstanding.

Not the best player in the league, Robinson was, however, a very shrewd one. He constantly plotted how to win the game, and studied and learned from teammates and opponents alike.

There were great players to learn from, some of the greatest in the Negro League. If white, they would also have been some of the greatest players in the major leagues. Among them were Satchel Paige, Josh Gibson, Buck Leonard, and Cool Papa Bell. Robinson watched them and learned, improving his skills in bunting, baserunning, and especially, base stealing.

Success on the diamond, however, did not make up for the misery of life in the Negro Leagues. When Robinson announced that he was quitting, the Monarchs enticed him to stay by raising his pay $25 a week. He, nevertheless, decided to quit at the end of the season, although he did not know what else he could do to earn enough money to support his mother and marry Rachel. Then a man named Branch Rickey summoned Jackie Robinson.

5

A TOE IN
THE DOOR

n August 28, 1945, a handsome young black man entered the Brooklyn, New York, offices of Branch Rickey, general manager of the Dodgers. He had been invited there to discuss a position with the Brooklyn Brown Dodgers, a new African-American baseball team that Rickey was supposed to be forming.

Branch Rickey peered at the visitor from under his bushy eyebrows, shook his hand vigorously, and greeted him in his deep booming voice. Rickey then got down to the real business of the meeting, which had nothing to do with the fictional Brown Dodgers.

He had studied the young man's career and personal life, Rickey explained, chomping on his cigar. "I think you can play in the major leagues," he added. "How do you feel about it?"[1] Jackie Robinson's answer would change the course of American sports history.

At the time of Robinson's historic meeting with Rickey, baseball had long been the national pastime. Yet African Americans, 10 percent of the population, were excluded from the major leagues.

People involved in baseball gave varied uninformed reasons for this ban:

- African Americans did not have the ability, the desire, or the intelligence to succeed in the majors, some argued. The skill and success of the players in the Negro Leagues poked holes in this argument.
- African-American players did not hone their skills in the minor leagues. Of course, these players were not admitted into the minor leagues.
- White players, especially those from the South, would not play with blacks. Polls, however, showed that most major leaguers did not object to integrated play, often playing on mixed teams in the off-season.
- Integrated teams would cause problems when they went South for spring training, because they would break Jim Crow laws aimed at enforcing segregation.

- Teams would lose money, because enraged white fans would not come to the games.

Perhaps the chief reason preventing integration, however, was that no one in baseball had had the courage to challenge custom, to take the risk, and to do it. Then along came Branch Rickey.

Sixty-three-year-old Branch Rickey had been in baseball most of his adult life and made many contributions to the game. He developed many of the training tools still used today, including sliding pits, batting tees, and a pitching machine. He also created the farm system, in which young players are signed to a minor league team and groomed until they are ready to play for the major league team that owns their contract.

With players off fighting in the war, and teams refusing to sign blacks, baseball limped along with white players who were too old or too young—even one-legged and one-armed. Newspapers and public figures began asking why African Americans were good enough to die for their country, but not good enough to play major league baseball. Committees formed to study how to integrate the sport.

In the spring of 1945 a few teams allowed African Americans to try out. Jackie Robinson was one of three players who tried out for the Boston Red Sox, even though he suspected that it was a setup to make the team look open to minority players. None of the three

When Branch Rickey chose Jackie Robinson to be the first African American to play major league baseball, he knew integration of the national pastime would be good for the country, good for baseball, and especially, good for the Dodgers.

heard from the Red Sox again. Boston would be the last major league team to integrate.

Joe Bostic, a newspaper reporter, arranged a player tryout with the Brooklyn Dodgers, even though he suspected it was also a waste of time. Bostic did not know that Branch Rickey felt that the time was right for change, and had already gained the approval of the Dodgers' other owners to integrate the team. Since people who supported segregation would try to stop such a move, Rickey kept his plans secret.

Why was Rickey the man with enough courage to attempt what he called his "noble experiment?" One reason is that Rickey knew it was the right thing to do. Years earlier, as baseball coach at Ohio Wesleyan University, he had seen the cruelty of prejudice firsthand. On a road trip a hotel refused to let first baseman Charley Thomas, an African American, stay at the hotel with the rest of the university team. Rickey talked the manager into letting Thomas share Rickey's room. He forever remembered the sight of the young man crying and rubbing his hands, wishing that they were white.

Rickey also knew that integrating baseball would be good for the country, good for baseball, and good for the Dodgers. With Negro Leaguers on his team, the Dodgers could be winners, and winners pull in fans—and money.

First, though, Rickey had to find the perfect

candidate to challenge the color barrier. He told his talent scouts to search for players for the mythical Brown Dodgers. The scouts spent two years observing over one hundred African-American players. Then they studied the lives, habits, reputations, and characters of thirty-six. One name appeared on every scout's list: Jack Roosevelt Robinson.

Dodger coach Clyde Sukeforth was very impressed with Robinson. Sukeforth called him a wonderful-looking athlete with broad shoulders and large hands, who chose his words carefully and spoke in a distinct cultured manner. He seemed to Sukeforth someone special, someone with determination and intelligence, who would not be pushed around.[2]

Robinson was not the best ballplayer considered, although his competitive skills made him a superb athlete. Rickey wanted more than a great player, however. "He wanted a player who could turn the other cheek and fight back by exceptional play," said Sukeforth. "He wanted a guy who could carry the flag of his race with his performance and his conduct."[3]

The one unanswered question was whether or not Jackie Robinson had the temperament to succeed as baseball's trailblazer. Could he stand the abuse and pressure that would come his way, yet still play well? If he did not play well, the plan would fail; if he did, no one could question an African American's right to be in the major leagues.

Rickey had heard stories of how Robinson's feisty nature got him into trouble, of how he always spoke up and fought back. Rickey had even traveled to California to research the tales of Robinson's temperament. He decided that if a white person had behaved the same way in those situations, his aggressiveness would have been admired.

Was Robinson *too* aggressive for Rickey's venture? Rickey had to find out. He pointed a finger at Robinson. "I know you're a good ballplayer," he barked. "What I don't know is whether you have the guts."[4] Then the stocky older man became an actor. For the next three hours, with sweat pouring off him, Rickey called Robinson every racist name he could think of. His cigar stabbed the air as he roleplayed the parts of the bigoted fan shrieking insults about Robinson's color and family, the hostile teammate turning his back on Robinson, the sadistic opponent sliding into base with his spikes aimed at Robinson's shins, and the stubborn hotel clerk refusing to give Robinson a room. By the time Rickey finished ranting at him, Robinson had his hands laced behind his back in fury.

Finally Robinson asked, "Mr. Rickey, are you looking for a Negro who is afraid to fight back?"

"Robinson," Rickey barked, "I'm looking for a ballplayer with guts enough not to fight back."[5] One incident, he explained, would set their cause back twenty years.

Robinson did not respond quickly. All his life he had believed in payback, in avenging insults, and that a person's most important asset was his dignity. Could he forget that and meekly accept abuse? It seemed impossible, but he knew he must do it—for African Americans, for Rachel, for his mother, and for himself.[6]

Finally, after a long silence, he told Rickey that if the older man were willing to take the gamble, there would be no incidents. Rickey then asked Robinson to turn the other cheek for three years, after which he was free to act as he wished.

Before the meeting ended, twenty-six-year-old Robinson agreed to play for the Montreal Royals, the Dodgers' top minor league farm club, for a $3,500 bonus and a salary of $600 a month.

Rickey chose Montreal because it was only one step from the Royals to the Dodgers and because it was in Canada. There, people accepted other races more willingly than in the United States. Robinson later wrote that Rickey's choice of Montreal could not have been better.[7]

For two months Robinson shared the secret of his future with only Rachel and his family. Then Rickey called a Montreal press conference for October 23, 1945.

With Robinson at his side, Hector Racine,

president of the Montreal club, told a roomful of reporters that Robinson was now a Royal. Although he later admitted being extremely nervous, Robinson looked calm and answered questions confidently, even smiling at times.[8]

Reaction to the news was swift. Some reports were critical of Rickey. They doubted that he truly wanted to end segregated baseball, but only wanted publicity. Some, especially reports from the South, protested the whole idea of mixed-race baseball.

Other writers questioned whether Robinson was the best choice. A few openly doubted that he had enough talent to make it in the big leagues. One sportswriter gave him only one chance in a thousand.[9] Some major league players agreed, stating that Robinson did not play well enough to be in their league, especially now that the star players were coming home from the war. Robinson's success thrilled Negro League players, but some were disappointed that they had not been chosen.

Many news reports, however, hailed the idea and likened Rickey to Abraham Lincoln. One reporter stated that as long as Robinson played well, fans would forget his race.[10] Other writers felt sorry for him because he had the hopes of millions of African Americans riding on his shoulders. The world watched and waited to see if that burden would make Jackie Robinson stumble and fall.

6

THE DOOR OPENS

ackie Robinson's stomach felt full of fireflies with claws.[1] It was April 18, 1946, and the Montreal Royals were opening their season against the Jersey City Giants. Fans, some from distant cities, had bought fifty-two thousand tickets. The Jersey City stadium held half that number. The press box overflowed with reporters. The diamond swarmed with photographers. Everyone had come to see the first African American in the twentieth century to play organized baseball.

On that opening day, Robinson had been a Royal for six months. It had been a busy six months.

Robinson had played winter ball in Venezuela for an all-star African-American team. He did not play his best, but he got valuable coaching from his teammates. They knew that if he made it in the big leagues, there was hope for them.

When he returned from South America, Jackie Robinson and Rachel Isum, who had dated off and on for six years, were married in Los Angeles on February 10, 1946.

The marriage began with some awkward incidents. On the way down the aisle, Robinson left his bride to visit with some old friends from the Pepper Street Gang.[2] Then members of the gang made off with the newlyweds' car, leaving them waiting until the jokers brought it back. When the young couple arrived at their hotel, they found that Robinson had forgotten to make reservations. These incidents seemed innocent fun compared to the experiences yet to come.

At the time of the wedding, racial unrest blanketed the nation, especially the South. Beatings, murders, and lynchings of African Americans still occurred. A few weeks after their honeymoon, the Robinsons headed for spring training in Daytona Beach, Florida.

The trip was a harsh introduction to Jim Crow laws. On a stopover in New Orleans, the Robinsons had to give up their airline seats to military personnel. This was common during war time, but the fighting was now over. Robinson called this, "Another typical black experience."[3] While waiting for the next open flight, the newlyweds learned that they could buy food from airport restaurants, but had to eat it elsewhere. The offended couple decided not to eat.

The delay stretched into hours. With no place at the airport for African Americans even to rest, Jackie and Rachel rented a room in a filthy downtown hotel. Twelve hours later they were again on their way, only to be bumped in Pensacola, Florida. This time a white couple took their seats.

Robinson was ready to explode, but he knew that would mean stories in the newspapers. Fighting back might also get him and Rachel arrested. Although it would have been easier to take a beating than to quietly accept such shameful treatment, Robinson swallowed his pride and his anger.[4]

Giving up on the airlines, the hungry couple boarded a Greyhound bus. For the next sixteen hours they sat crammed into overcrowded straight-back seats at the rear of the bus or stood, staring at empty reclining seats reserved for white passengers. The thought of how humiliated her husband must feel made Rachel want to weep; the thought of how humiliated his bride must feel made Jackie want to quit.[5]

Although the Robinsons had to stay with a prominent African-American family and not at the hotel with the team, Daytona Beach accepted the new Royal. Not so the nearby town of Sanford, where the Royals held practices.

The first day that Robinson arrived at the Sanford ballpark, the crowd around the front gate was so hostile that he found a hole in the fence and entered through it. When Sanford town officials told Branch Rickey that blacks and whites would not be allowed on the same field, Rickey moved the entire operation back to Daytona Beach.

Fortunately, Robinson's teammates were less threatening. At first the other Royals were neither hostile nor friendly. Robinson kept to himself and did not speak unless spoken to. Whenever a teammate did approach him, Robinson made him feel comfortable. Slowly the white players became less distant and even began sharing hints to improve the rookie's play.

Robinson began at shortstop. Eager to do his best, he threw as hard as he could. His arm became so sore that he could not lift it. Rickey moved him to second base, a position that did not need such a powerful throwing arm.

Robinson felt anxious before the first exhibition game between the Royals and their parent club, the Dodgers. He expected a chorus of jeers and taunts. Instead the cheers drowned out the few scattered boos. His confidence returned, but the endless pressure kept him from playing his best. A reporter later wrote that a white player showing Robinson's poor skills would have been booted out of spring training long before.[6]

The exhibition games that followed were upsetting in other ways. Towns canceled games or locked up their ballparks when the Royals arrived. A daytime game was canceled with the feeble excuse that the lights needed repair. In Sanford, Robinson played two innings before the chief of police arrived. He told the Royals' manager that Robinson could not even sit on the bench, but had to leave the park.

Branch Rickey at first had planned not to push his new player on any city that resented his presence. Now he decided that if Jackie Robinson did not play, the Royals did not play. He moved the team's out-of-town games to Daytona Beach. There, brave city officials ignored local laws and allowed interracial games.

By April Robinson's play was improving, but his nerves had taken such a beating that he could not sleep or relax. Then came April 18, opening day against the Jersey City Giants.

Robinson's knees felt wobbly and his hands too damp to hold the bat properly.[7] Still he managed four hits (one a three-run homer), scored four runs, and drove in three more to lead the Royals to a 14–1 win. He displayed his excellent bunting skills, but what thrilled the fans most was his baserunning.

Using tactics Negro Leaguers called "trickeration,"

Robinson terrorized pitchers and catchers.[8] He often did this on third base. On and off the base he danced, one minute toward home, then back to third. These planned antics upset the pitcher, making him lose concentration. Often the pitcher let Robinson steal or he balked. A balk means that the pitcher pauses too long after his windup or stretch, or fakes a throw with one foot still on the part of the mound called the rubber. Balks are not allowed. The penalty is that all base runners advance one base. Sometimes Robinson walked home. This baserunning talent became his trademark, delighting fans for years to come.

Robinson was not simply trying to annoy the pitcher with his "trickeration," however. He was timing how long it took the pitcher to throw the ball home. After a few tries, he knew how close he needed to be to home plate to beat the ball there. His skill and savvy on the diamond impressed fans and reporters alike. Suddenly newspapers were calling him a "real" ballplayer.

Perhaps more important to Robinson than this praise were two incidents that occurred during the opening game. They would be minor events in most baseball games, but meant a lot to the first African American in the modern major leagues. After Robinson's home run, Montreal manager Clay Hopper patted Robinson on the back as he rounded third base. After Robinson scored, Royals' outfielder

George Shuba shook his hand. The next day the first photo of a black player being congratulated by a white teammate for a home run appeared in the newspaper.

Manager Clay Hopper's pat on the back was even more remarkable. Although he was always civil to Robinson, Hopper, from Mississippi, had been distressed when asked to coach an African American.[9] One time, when Branch Rickey had described one of Robinson's catches as "superhuman," Hopper had asked, "Do you really think a nigger's a human being?"[10]

After his superb play in Jersey City, Robinson relaxed somewhat, but the Royals had two weeks on the road before their first game in Montreal. It was a difficult time. While his fellow Royals remained cordial, the team's sleeping arrangements were segregated, and the men still did not go out of their way to interact with Robinson.

Players on rival teams went out of their way to torment him. Runners slid into second with their spikes high. Pitchers aimed at his head. Players booed and jeered when he stepped up to the plate, yelled racial insults, and in Syracuse, New York, even pushed a black cat onto the field and called it Robinson's cousin.

In Baltimore, Maryland, the last stop before going to Montreal, rumors flew of a fan boycott. Only 3,415 fans showed up for the first game, but those few gave

Robinson such a tongue-lashing that Rachel, sitting in the stands, feared for his safety. The next night, over twenty-five hundred fans raised their voices in scorn.

Montreal provided a vivid contrast. The city welcomed the Robinsons and made them feel at home. They found an apartment in the French-speaking area of town and were fondly accepted by their neighbors. Hometown crowds adored Robinson. They shouted encouragement at him, thrilled by the daring way he played.

Robinson responded. Even though injuries, most of them to his legs from baserunners, made him sit out some games, he led the International League in hitting with .349, was second in stolen bases, tied with another player in runs scored, was the best fielder among second basemen in the league, and was named the league's Most Valuable Player.

Still the pressure of being a groundbreaker in baseball remained intense. At home, Rachel was now pregnant with the couple's first child, due in late autumn. When Robinson began to have trouble sleeping and eating, a doctor decided the ballplayer was near a nervous breakdown and told him to take off ten days. Worried that people would think that he was trying to protect his batting record, Robinson returned a few days later and helped the Royals clinch the International League pennant.[11] The team won the playoffs and faced the Louisville Colonels in the minor league's Junior World Series.

The first three games of the series were in Louisville, Kentucky. The opener was the first interracial game played in that southern city in this century. Eager African-American fans, not allowed to buy all the tickets they wanted, climbed or clung to any handy high point outside the ballpark to get a glimpse of their champion.

The games in Louisville were a test of Robinson's ability to tolerate abuse. The Colonels had been warned not to badger Robinson during the games. Yet their fans received no such advice. With every move Robinson made, he felt waves of hatred rushing from the stands toward him.[12]

Robinson endured the torment, but his play suffered. He got only one hit. Without Robinson zipping around the bases in his pigeon-toed gait, the Royals lost two of the three games. They had to win three of the next four to take the series. Luckily the games were to be played in Montreal.

The hometown fans gave back to the Colonels what the Louisville fans had heaped on Montreal's Jackie. The crowd eagerly jeered and booed the Colonels. The love of the Montreal fans worked like a tonic for the Royals. Robinson came out of his slump and played like a superstar. In the next three games he got seven hits for a series batting average of .400. The Royals won those games—and the championship.

Elated fans poured onto the field. They chanted Robinson's name. They hoisted him to their shoulders and paraded him, singing, around the field. They waited outside the locker room until he had showered and changed. Then they hugged him. They kissed him. They refused to let him go. Finally Robinson broke through the throng and ran down the street, the cheering crowd following. A reporter for the *Pittsburgh Courier* wrote that "it was probably the only day in history that a black man ran from a white mob with love instead of lynching on its mind."[13]

The acclaim thrilled Robinson, but something that happened in the locker room after the game was probably just as satisfying. Manager Clay Hopper, the man who had wondered if Robinson was human, shook his hand, then said, "You're a great ballplayer and a fine gentleman. It's been wonderful having you on the team."[14]

7

LAMB WITH A
LION'S HEART

It was the middle of a spring night in Panama, where the Brooklyn Dodgers and the Montreal Royals were playing some 1947 pre-season exhibition games. In the kitchen behind the Dodgers' mess hall, weary players sat slumped on counters or leaned against refrigerators and stoves.

Their manager, Leo Durocher, standing before them in his yellow bathrobe, had rousted them from their beds. He had heard that some Dodgers were signing a petition to stop Jackie Robinson from joining the team, even though Branch Rickey had made no statement about bringing Robinson up from the Royals. News about coming to the majors usually was announced over the winter, but Rickey was still proceeding very carefully with his plan to integrate major league ball.

To avoid the racial problems Florida had presented, Rickey had moved spring training to Cuba. There, races mixed freely and people idolized Robinson. In Cuba, however, Rickey made a mistake. In a country where Robinson could live and eat with his team, Rickey arranged for Robinson and the three other African Americans who had joined the Dodgers' minor league teams—Roy Campanella, Don Newcombe, and Roy Partlow—to live in a separate seedy hotel. Rickey thought that this would reduce tension among the players. The white Royals, at a newly-built military academy, and the Dodgers, at a deluxe hotel, dined on steaks flown in from the mainland. Robinson and his companions received a meal allowance to spend at local restaurants.

Rickey hoped only to avoid racial incidents among team members, but instead, he caused problems for his African-American players. None spoke good Spanish, so they could not communicate their needs. Also the local food, often unsanitary, made them ill, especially Robinson, who particularly resented the arrangements.[1]

Rickey had set up plenty of games between the

Royals and the Dodgers, so the Dodger players could see how brilliantly Robinson played. When they realized that Robinson could help them win, the players would beg Rickey to move him up to their club. Newspapers would spread the word, too, and fans would clamor for Robinson to join the Dodgers.

Even though the ailing Robinson batted over .500 in games against the Dodgers, he was again learning a new position—first base—and still looked awkward there. So neither the Dodgers nor the fans demanded that he be moved up. Instead a few Dodgers from the South started the petition to keep Robinson off the team.

These players did not hate Jackie Robinson, but they had been taught that races should not mix. They truly believed that they could not play on a team with an African American. Then Dodgers' manager Leo Durocher heard about the petition.

At the mess hall meeting that night, Durocher told the players that he did not care if a man was yellow or black or had stripes like a zebra. If Durocher said he could play, he would play. Besides, if Robinson did move up, he would make them all rich. Any Dodger who did not like the idea of playing with the man could ask to be traded to another team.[2] There were two takers.

The petition probably would have been doomed even if Durocher had not learned of it. Most northerners, and even some southerners—including Pete Reiser, and shortstop and team leader Pee Wee Reese—refused to sign. The petition threat proved, however, that the players would not beg Rickey to make Robinson a Dodger. Rickey needed a new plan.

Then on April 9, 1947, Leo Durocher was suspended from baseball for one year for spending time with known gamblers, behavior thought harmful to the sport.

While the public uproar about the suspension swirled, Rickey acted swiftly. That afternoon, during an exhibition game between the Royals and the Dodgers, a notice appeared on the bulletin board in the press box, the area where sportswriters watch and report on the game. The notice read that the Brooklyn Dodgers had purchased the contract of Jackie Robinson from the Montreal Royals, effective immediately.

Word passed quickly to the field, where Robinson was at bat. Returning to the dugout, he probably wondered why Clay Hopper and his Royal teammates were grinning, clapping, and giving him thumbs-up signs. He had just bunted into a double play, and two outs were nothing to cheer. He soon understood their behavior. Branch Rickey had kept his word. Robinson was now a Brooklyn Dodger. Was the worst over . . . or yet to come?

Jackie Roosevelt Robinson, now twenty-eight,

At a 1947 exhibition game between the Montreal Royals and the Brooklyn Dodgers only days before he became a Dodger, young fans beg Robinson for an autograph.

made his debut in major league baseball as number 42 for the Brooklyn Dodgers on April 15, 1947. Rachel and five-month-old Jackie, Jr., who had been born in November, were in the Brooklyn stands that cool rainy day. Even though Robinson had no hits, he fielded well at first base and helped the Dodgers defeat the Boston Braves, 5–3.

Most remarkable about that game was how unremarkable it was. Except for the one dark face on the field and the larger-than-usual number of African-American fans in the crowd—14,000 out of 26,623—nothing happened to make this opening day different from any other.[3]

The next few games were also routine. Robinson got his first major league hit in the second game and hit his first major league home run in the third. Then the Philadelphia Phillies came to Brooklyn, and Robinson endured the name calling that nearly made him crack, but also saw his teammates rise to his defense.

Despite his teammates' support, Robinson did not immediately become a fully accepted member of the Dodgers. In the meantime, he continued the policy that he had started with Montreal: He kept to himself unless invited to join the other players' activities. After games he waited to shower until the other players finished. On road trips he read or stared out the window. He ate alone. Although one sportswriter

Wearing his Montreal Royal uniform for the last time, Robinson enters the Brooklyn clubhouse to become a Brooklyn Dodger and the first African American in the major leagues.

called him the loneliest man in sports, his relationship with his teammates was likely one of Robinson's lesser worries.[4]

Early in the season he went into a slump, getting only one hit in twenty tries, and was in danger of getting benched. Rival players kicked or spiked him. Pitchers planted themselves on the baseline to tag him out instead of simply throwing the ball to first base. Nine pitches hit Robinson that season, but because of his agility, never on the head. A few times Robinson made a move to fight back, then, mustering his willpower and heeding Rickey's plea for self-control, stopped himself.

Robinson received a flood of encouraging letters, but also letters threatening the lives and safety of him and his family. One letter, threatening to kill him if he played in Cincinnati, was taken so seriously that the FBI searched the rooftops and upper stories of all buildings near the ballpark.

May 9, 1947, was probably one of the worst days of Robinson's baseball career. Upon arriving in Philadelphia for a series against the Phillies, the hotel where the Dodgers usually stayed refused to accept him. That same day the New York *Herald Tribune* announced that the St. Louis Cardinals had threatened to strike when the Dodgers came to town. The Cardinals denied this. A pitcher for the Chicago Cubs, however, said that he believed that *all* the teams

Robinson clutches his arm after being hit with a ball thrown by a New York Giant pitcher. Opposing pitchers often threw at Robinson when he came up to bat. In his first season, he was hit nine times.

were voting on whether or not to strike against the interracial team.[5]

During that day's game against Philadelphia, the Phillies continued the torment they had begun in Brooklyn the month before. Spurred on by the death threats that Robinson had received, they even pointed bats at him and made machine gun noises.

Worse yet, Rickey had asked Robinson to pose for a photograph of him shaking hands with Ben Chapman, the man who had directed the first Phillies' attack. Public opinion was so much against Chapman that he was in danger of losing his job. The Phillies' management thought that it would be helpful if the two were pictured making peace. Although he admitted that it was one of the most difficult acts he had ever done, Robinson agreed.[6]

Chapman, however, refused to shake hands, so the photograph shows the two men holding a bat, Chapman with two hands on the bat, Robinson with one.

Robinson sometimes wondered if his effort to integrate baseball was worth it, especially after the humiliating photo shoot with Chapman.[7] Around this time he telephoned his family in Pasadena and told them that he was quitting. His mother and his brother Mack persuaded him to stay.[8]

It was one of the few times Robinson revealed what he was feeling. His teammates and the Dodgers' management never knew. Even with his wife, Robinson shared little. Although Rachel tried to get him to talk about the problems he faced, he did not want to worry her, so he kept silent. At night, however, he jerked and twitched and talked in his sleep, so Rachel knew that her husband was a troubled man.[9]

The Robinsons had been living in a Manhattan hotel. With a baby and no cooking or washing facilities, this was an impossible situation. When they moved to a small apartment in Brooklyn, it was not much better. It had only a bedroom, a sleeping area for Jackie, Jr., and the use of a shared kitchen.

Despite all these challenges, Robinson began to come out of his slump and hit the ball. Wherever he played, huge crowds turned out, setting attendance records. Thousands of these fans were African Americans, who often traveled hundreds of miles by bus or train to attend.

The large numbers of African Americans pleased Robinson, but also pressured him to perform well to thank them for their support.[10] At times the enthusiasm of these avid fans embarrassed him, however, especially when they cheered everything he did—whether a home run or an easy-out ball.[11] Sometimes their behavior even infuriated him.[12] In one incident, a few years after he joined the Dodgers, some white police officers opened a section of white

As a Brooklyn Dodger, Robinson played his home games at
Ebbets Field. Four years after Robinson's last game as a Dodger,
Ebbets Field was torn down.

seats to black fans with no place to sit. The blacks cheered.

"Don't cheer!" Robinson yelled, throwing down his glove and pacing in a tight circle. "You got it coming. You're only getting what's coming. . . . Don't cheer!"[13]

Pride in their fellow black gained Robinson the support of black fans. Slowly Robinson also gained the support of white fans, and eventually, of his teammates. It was not simply his ability to help the Dodgers win games that won the team over. It was also Robinson's personality and conduct—his intelligence, his sense of humor, his ability to understand and forgive his tormentors, and perhaps most of all, his determination to behave like a lamb when, at heart, he was really a lion.

Pee Wee Reese was the first Dodger to befriend Robinson. Reese showed his support in a game the following year. Fans and bench jockeys taunted Robinson and mocked Reese for being his friend. Reese said nothing; he simply walked over to first base and put his arm around Robinson, silencing the jeers.

Robinson's love of card games also helped him connect with his teammates. Gradually he joined in the gin rummy, poker, and bridge games that the others played.

Then one day in June teammate Al Gionfriddo told him that the rule that blacks could not shower with whites did not apply in their clubhouse, and

During his first year as a Dodger, Robinson played the infield with (left to right) Johnny (Spider) Jorgensen, Pee Wee Reese, and Eddie Stanky. Reese was the first Dodger to befriend Robinson.

Robinson got up and took a shower with the rest of the team.[14]

As his relations with fellow players improved, so did Robinson's play. He was near the top of the league in hitting, scoring, and base stealing, and led the Dodgers in home runs. Although some racism from fans still occurred, abusive treatment from rival players lessened when they learned that Robinson simply took his anger and channeled it into his performance. Phillie player Richie Ashburn said that Robinson was a fearless player who could not be intimidated.[15] Most opposing teams quit trying.

The 1947 Brooklyn Dodgers won the National League pennant, and Jackie Robinson was named the Baseball Writers' Association's first Rookie of the Year. In 1987 Commissioner Peter Ueberroth would name the award after Jackie Robinson.

In September Brooklyn hosted a Jackie Robinson Day at Ebbets Field, home of the Dodgers. Mallie Robinson watched as fans gave her son $10,000 worth of gifts, including a Cadillac and a television set. His salary that year had been $5,000, the lowest a major leaguer could be paid.

Soon after, Jackie Robinson became the first African American to play in a World Series. The Dodgers lost the series to the New York Yankees, but it had been an outstanding season for the rookie.

Dixie Walker, who had signed the petition and

chosen to be traded when Robinson became a Dodger, asked Rickey to forget the trade. Even Phillies' manager Ben Chapman admitted that Robinson was, in all respects, a major leaguer.[16]

A public opinion poll taken around that time named Robinson the second most popular man in America, after the singer/actor Bing Crosby.

Robinson stated, "I had started the season as a lonely man. . . . I ended it feeling like a member of a solid team."[17] He and the Dodgers had both learned something. Robinson learned self-control and how to earn the respect of his teammates. The Dodgers learned that performance counts more than skin color. Maybe, Robinson added, "the bigots had learned that, too."[18]

Not only was 1947 an outstanding season for Robinson, it was also a banner year for baseball. Thanks to Robinson, crowds set attendance records in every city except Cincinnati. Even more important, Negro Leaguer Larry Doby had signed with the Cleveland Indians of the American League. The door Jackie Robinson had nudged open now hung off its hinges.

8

THE LION ROARS

Although the door to major league baseball was now open to African Americans, few footsteps echoed along the path behind Jackie Robinson. By 1953 only six of the sixteen major league teams had integrated. In January 1957 three teams still had no African Americans. The Boston Red Sox were the last club to integrate, doing so in 1959. In the meantime Robinson continued to meet new challenges.

When he reported to spring training in 1948, Robinson was overweight and out of shape. He had spent much of the winter break on a speaking tour, eating too much at banquets and at the homes of friendly hosts. Manager Leo Durocher, back from his year's suspension, made insulting remarks to the press about Robinson's weight, and had him exercise and practice in a rubber suit. Although Robinson later admitted that Durocher was only doing his job, at the time, he resented such treatment.[1] He did not play well that spring.

That summer the Robinsons moved into a larger apartment in Brooklyn, and Leo Durocher left the Dodgers for the New York Giants. Around the same time Robinson's play improved. It was a coincidence, but an angry Durocher thought that Robinson had not given him his best effort.[2]

In September Robinson heckled an umpire about a strike called against another Dodger. The umpire threw Robinson out of the game. Instead of being angry, Robinson felt great, because the ump had treated him just as he would any ballplayer who annoyed him.[3] Robinson considered it the most important event that happened to him in 1948.[4]

An event that had more impact on Robinson's life occurred soon after. For three years—first as a Royal, then as a Dodger—Branch Rickey had watched Robinson hold his tongue and hold his temper. He knew that the tension of doing so was taking a toll on the young man. Believing his experiment with integration was successful, Rickey told Robinson that he was now free to be himself.

Although the Dodgers finished third in 1948, Robinson, playing second base, had a good year on and off the diamond. In New York, Rudolph Thomas, director of the Harlem YMCA, asked Robinson to be the Y's youth director during the off-season. Most of the Y's young people were African Americans. Robinson believed that his words and accomplishments could inspire them. He believed that they, in turn, might change society. For the next decade Robinson coached and advised these youngsters.

When Robinson arrived at spring training in 1949, lean and ready to play, he immediately let everyone know that the meek lamb was history. The lion had arrived. "They'd better be rough on me this year," he announced, "because I'm sure going to be rough on them."[5]

Robinson meant that he was going to play hard and not accept any abusive treatment, but for the rest of his baseball career Robinson was glorified for his playing ability and criticized for speaking out.

Although Robinson had always spoken his mind before joining the Dodgers, the pressure of keeping his true nature bottled up for three years probably made him more vocal than usual. He sparred with reporters, protested calls, and argued with umpires. He exchanged words with opposing players and coaches. When the Dodgers played the Giants, Robinson's verbal clashes with Giants' manager Leo Durocher became famous.

Using the baserunning skills that were his trademark and that thrilled fans and tormented rival players, Robinson tries to steal home against the Chicago Cubs.

While he did not curb his tongue, Robinson did control his actions. He never got into any physical fights or any quarrels that affected the outcome of the game. Winning was too important. Yet the criticism of him, much of it in the newspapers, was frequent and loud.

Beginning in 1949 Robinson had a love-hate relationship with the press. Reporters were eager to interview Robinson because he was open and honest with answers. That honesty got him into trouble when he talked about social issues or even when he simply squawked about an unfair call. Then the reports were disapproving, sometimes even untrue.

One day the Dodgers lost a close game on an umpire's bad call. The team was furious and griped loudly, none more loudly than Robinson. His high-pitched voice, which got even higher when he was angry, was easy to recognize. An eavesdropping reporter with a looming deadline heard, but did not see, pitcher Preacher Roe kick a hole in the umpires' dressing room door as the team passed. That evening a newspaper headline announced that Robinson had lost his temper and kicked in the door.

Rachel Robinson believed that some of the disputes between her husband and the press occurred because reporters wanted to discuss the game, but Robinson wanted to talk about social issues, especially racial inequality.[6]

The excitement of watching Jackie Robinson try to steal a base shows on the face of his wife Rachel (center).

Robinson believed that he was criticized more than other players, not because he spoke out more, but simply because he was an African American who spoke out. As long as he ignored the insults and injuries, Robinson said, people saw him as the heroic underdog. When he said what he thought, he became a "pop-off," a "sorehead," an "uppity nigger." A white player behaving the same way "had spirit."[7]

Sportswriter Dick Young, who had an uneasy relationship with Robinson, accused him of being too sensitive about his race, of thinking everything bad that happened to him was because he was African American.[8] Vince Scully, the broadcaster for the Dodgers, reported one such incident.

The Dodgers had just finished a game against the Phillies. As the Dodgers left the Philadelphia stadium that sweltering day, an old shabby fan outside the gate handed pieces of watermelon to the players as they boarded their bus. The rest of the team had already boarded when Robinson appeared. The man held out the watermelon to Robinson, who thought he was being mocked, the way the police had mocked the Pepper Street Gang when they complained of thirst. Furious, he spoke harshly to the man, only to board the bus, and see his teammates eating watermelon, and realize he had misjudged the fan's intentions.

Dick Young also told Robinson that when he spoke to Roy Campanella, next to Robinson the most famous

African-American player of the time, he never thought of Campanella as an African American. When he spoke to Robinson, Young was always very aware that Robinson was African American.[9]

Robinson probably intended it to be that way. As a major league baseball player, Robinson felt the pressure of representing his race. He had become a spokesperson for his people, a national hero, and an important historical figure. He wanted Dick Young to be aware that he was not speaking to just another ballplayer.

Some newspapers, however, stated that Robinson should remember that he *was* just a baseball player, not a symbol, and should stick to baseball business. Other newspapers claimed he *was* a symbol—a symbol of integration, a symbol whose behavior should be above criticism.

Robinson knew that he was a baseball player *and* a symbol, but he did not think being obedient and grateful fulfilled his role. African-American leaders, he believed, should be demanding and outspoken. Proud and defiant, he told Dick Young that he was not going to beg for anything, that he was reasonable, but "tired of being patient."[10] He saw the integration of baseball as the beginning of important changes in society itself. He felt obligated to help those reforms come about.

Despite being criticized by sportswriters for airing

his opinions, on one occasion in 1949, Robinson earned praise across the country for doing so.

Around that time, many Americans were worried that communism was becoming too popular in the United States. One belief of communist doctrine is that there should be no private property, that everything in a country should be owned by everyone. Communists spoke out against discrimination, and had often called for the integration of such national pastimes as baseball. This made communism appealing to many people. Most people, however, saw it as a threat to democracy. The government had even set up a group called the House Un-American Activities Committee (HUAC) to investigate communism.

Paul Robeson, once a college football player, had become a famous singer and actor. He was also African American. In the spring of 1949 he announced that African Americans would never fight a war against the Soviet Union because that communist country treated people of his race with dignity and opposed racism, whereas America oppressed minorities.

HUAC decided another famous African American should speak out against Robeson. They asked thirty-year-old Jackie Robinson. Robinson knew and respected Robeson, and Robeson had been one of the first public figures to call for the integration of baseball.

HUAC, however, pressured Robinson to speak, and Branch Rickey urged him to cooperate. Finally, on July 18, 1949, Robinson appeared before the committee in Washington, D.C. In his statement, he said that Robeson did not speak for all African Americans. Neither did he, Robinson, but even though it was not perfect, he would fight for his country. He would also keep fighting to end discrimination and segregation in America.[11] Newspapers praised Robinson for his support of democracy. His testimony, however, helped ruin the reputation, career, and life of Robeson.

Years later Robinson wrote that he never regretted his testimony rejecting communism and racism.[12] He did, however, regret speaking out against Robeson. He had more faith in 1949 than he had in 1960 that white America would offer justice to its black citizens.[13]

After his testimony Robinson immediately returned to New York, and that evening hit a triple to propel him toward his best year in baseball. By the season's end Robinson led the league in hitting, stolen bases, and double plays, and was the first African American named the National League's Most Valuable Player.

Once more the Dodgers won the pennant and met the Yankees in the World Series. Although the Dodgers lost, it was a winning season for Robinson, who was again able to roar.

9

STORMING THE
BARRICADES

ackie and Rachel Robinson entered the dining room of the Netherlands-Plaza Hotel in Cincinnati. The hotel allowed African Americans to stay there, but tradition required them to eat meals in their rooms, never in the dining room. Robinson had had enough of that custom. By the early 1950s he had been a Dodger for several years. He deserved to eat where the white players ate.

The maître d' led them to a table and vanished. He returned moments later with a baseball and pen. He had been waiting all season, he said, for Robinson to eat in the dining room so that he could get his autograph.[1]

Robinson had stormed another barricade. During his ten years with the Dodgers, he never stopped.

Early in 1950 Robinson spent time in Hollywood filming the story of his life, one of the first movies about an African-American hero. He refused to begin filming until the birth of his second child, daughter Sharon, who was born on January 13. *The Jackie Robinson Story* took only a few months to complete and opened in May 1950. Robinson earned $50,000, plus a share of the movie's profits.

That year Robinson's baseball salary jumped too. In 1949 it was $13,000. In 1950 it leaped to $35,000, more than any Dodger had ever been paid. Still the money flowed in. He made commercials for products such as bread and canned milk. He did radio programs, wrote a newspaper column, and made personal appearances. There were Jackie Robinson jackets, caps, and watches. The Jackie Robinson Clothing Store sold quality clothes with his name on the label.

The Dodgers had a disappointing year in 1950, losing the pennant to Philadelphia. That year Robinson received another serious death threat, which again brought out the FBI. This time the manager shared the threat with the other Dodgers. One player suggested that they all wear Robinson's number 42 on their uniforms. Then the killer would not know which one to shoot. The humor helped ease the tension, but it also showed that when Robinson had a problem, the team now experienced it with him.

As the seasons passed, Robinson became the focus of the team. It was Robinson who made new players, black or white, feel welcome. When the Giants traded pitcher Sal "the Barber" Maglie to the Dodgers, he did not know how he would be received. Over the years he and Robinson had feuded intensely. Maglie threw at Robinson. Robinson bunted down the first baseline so that he could run down Maglie when he fielded the ball. When Maglie walked into his new clubhouse, however, the first Dodger to welcome him was Jackie Robinson.

Robinson went out of his way to help rookie African Americans play their best. Don Newcombe pitched better when he was angry, so Robinson goaded him until he got riled. Joe Black pitched better when he stayed calm, so Robinson quieted him down. Determined to help any African American in baseball succeed, he even shared advice with players on opposing teams. He sometimes gave Willie Mays of the Giants hints on hitting certain pitchers—not Dodger pitchers though.

As more African Americans joined the majors, Robinson began calling for them to be hired as managers, coaches, and field and office personnel. He ordered those joining his team not to sit together at one table or to choose lockers side by side, so they would not look like a "spot."[2]

Robinson's locker was not far from that of shortstop Pee Wee Reese. The two Dodgers became the best double play twosome in baseball, and their professional relationship grew into a genuine friendship.

The 1951 season began badly for Robinson. He had lost his personal champion. At the end of the 1950 season Branch Rickey, needing the money, had sold his share of the Dodgers to Walter O'Malley, now president and general manager. O'Malley had never liked Rickey. He began fining any Dodger who spoke Rickey's name one dollar. Robinson, in turn, had no love for anyone who did not respect Branch Rickey.

Still Robinson put his heart into every game. At the end of the season the Dodgers needed one win against Philadelphia to tie for the pennant. After nine innings the score was 8–8. In the bottom of the twelfth inning a Phillies player smacked the ball toward center field, which would bring in the winning run. Robinson, playing second, made what many fans consider one of the greatest defensive plays in baseball. He launched himself into the air, his body and glove outstretched. As he landed, his elbow jammed into his ribs and stomach. Though nearly knocked unconscious, he made the catch.

Hurting badly, Robinson doubted that he could keep playing, but he did. Two innings later he hit a home run to win the game.

After the Dodgers lost the pennant playoffs to the Giants, Robinson went to the New York clubhouse to congratulate the players and their manager, Leo Durocher. He was the only Dodger to do so.

Durocher knew how difficult this gesture would be for any losing player. "Jackie Robinson had class," Durocher said later. "He was some man."[3]

The year 1952 did not end without Robinson creating controversy. While appearing on the television show *Youth Wants To Know*, a young woman asked Robinson if he thought that the New York Yankees, still an all-white team, were prejudiced against African-American players. Robinson said yes. A storm of protest swirled around him after that remark, with the Yankees team defending its position, and Robinson defending his.

During his years with the Dodgers, Robinson never stopped battling racism. Don Newcombe, who joined the Dodgers in 1949, called Robinson a forerunner in the civil rights movement. When people saw what Robinson accomplished in the face of such odds, said Newcombe, they realized that they could accomplish much in their own lives.[4]

In 1953, around the time that he integrated the dining room of the Netherlands-Plaza, Robinson also became the first African American to stay at the Chase Hotel in St. Louis, the last major league city to end segregation in hotels and ballparks. The hotel had agreed to let the African-American Dodgers sleep at the Chase, but they could not use the dining room, the nightclub, the swimming pool, or linger in the lobby.

The other African-American players chose to stay loyal to the black hotel that had treated them well over the years. Robinson accepted the Chase's offer. The door had opened a crack. Robinson knew that once he had his toe in, that door, too, would swing wide.

A year later he and Newcombe challenged the hotel manager to let them eat in the dining room. The manager agreed. The hotel found other ways to discriminate though. African Americans were given dark out-of-the-way rooms with no view, and received especially slow service in the dining room and nightclub. Robinson did not give up. He kept staying at the Chase until the hotel's official policy changed a few years later.

Robinson believed that baseball could have done more to end discrimination in housing and services, especially in the South. Teams spent millions of dollars training there every year. If ball clubs threatened to take their business elsewhere, as a few finally did, change would come more rapidly.[5]

The Dodgers' management did not abandon spring training in Florida, but by 1949 the club had built a private training facility in Vero Beach, where players of all races roomed and ate together—a tiny island of tolerance in an ocean of bigotry.

10

AN OLD GRAY
FAT MAN

 s Robinson's baseball career began to wind down, his importance as a public figure grew. Famous people—including General Douglas MacArthur and comedians Jonathan Winters and Danny Kaye—often showed up at the Dodgers' clubhouse, hoping to meet Robinson. President Dwight Eisenhower asked to be introduced. Robinson was also friendly with Thurgood Marshall and Kenneth B. Clark, Justices of the Supreme Court. He met a young civil rights leader named Martin Luther King, Jr., who called Robinson an inspiration. Without

Robinson's example, King said, he would never have been able to do what he did.[1]

As well-known as he was, Robinson still faced discrimination. The family was now living in its own house in a mixed-race, middle-class neighborhood in Queens, New York. Fans constantly rang the doorbell, wanting autographs or the family to pose for photos. After another son, David, was born in May 1952, the Robinsons wanted to move to a larger home, where they would have more room and more privacy.

Rachel and Jackie began looking for a house outside the city. Desirable houses suddenly disappeared from the market or else their price zoomed out of reach—signs that the neighborhoods did not want African Americans, even famous ones, moving in. Then a newspaper published an article on the Robinson's frustrating house search. Stung by the criticism, one community formed a committee to help the family. The Robinsons soon owned five acres with a private lake in Stamford, Connecticut. In 1955, three years after they began their search, the Robinsons moved into the new twelve-room, redwood-and-fieldstone home that they had planned and built.

In 1954 Robinson had begun to think of retiring from baseball. He did not get along with the new manager, Walter Alston, who cut his playing time and moved him from one position to another. A few times the two were prevented from coming to blows only because other players stepped in to stop the spat.

Also, although only thirty-five, Robinson no longer had the strong athlete's body he had when younger. His hair was going gray; his knees were bad. His body had taken a beating from football tackles, from baserunners, and from pitchers. Rough games were not the only reason that he was in such poor shape. Robinson had developed Type II diabetes, a condition caused by the body's inability to make enough of the hormone called insulin.

His gray hair and a roll of fat around his middle soon earned Robinson the nickname "the old gray fat man."[2] His speed around the bases was mostly a memory. At a game in St. Louis late in his career, one elderly fan, watching Robinson run the bases, commented, "Oh Jackie, you ain't what you used to was [sic]."[3]

In 1955, nagged with injuries and still at odds with his manager, he sat on the bench most of the season, hitting under .300 for the first time since 1948. The 1955 Dodgers nevertheless won the pennant. For the fifth time Robinson again faced the Yankees in the World Series.

His statistics for the series are poor, and he sat out the final game. Robinson was, however, the ballplayer who Ralph Kiner described as the "only player I ever saw who could completely turn a game around by himself."[4] So those numbers do not tell how Robinson sparked his team with his daring, how he used his battered legs and his lion's heart to create runs when they were most needed. Robinson even stole home against Yankee catcher Yogi Berra, who had bragged that no one, not even Jackie Robinson, could steal home when Berra was on the plate.[5] Robinson's steal, together with his "trickeration," set his team on fire. In 1955 the Dodgers gave Brooklyn its only World Series Championship.

Jackie Robinson may have been thirty-six years old, tired, gray, and overweight, but his four hits and five runs came when his team most needed them. Typically, Robinson gave credit for winning to Reese, Campanella, Snider, and the managing of Walter Alston.

In 1956 Robinson, injured and not well, played as hard as he could. He helped lead the team to another pennant, only to lose again to the Yankees in the seventh game of the series.

During the winter Robinson heard rumors that the Dodgers might be leaving Brooklyn for Los Angeles, and that he might be traded. He wondered if he should retire. Some events helped him decide.

First he signed a $50,000 contract with *Look* magazine. The contract said *Look* would announce the story of Robinson's retirement—whenever it occurred. Usually an athlete would tell his general manager, then hold an open news conference to inform the media. Now Robinson could not do this until *Look* printed the story.

Robinson shares a quiet moment at home with his family in Stamford, Connecticut, shortly before his retirement from baseball. From left to right are David, four; Rachel; Jackie, Jr., ten; and Sharon, seven.

Next, on December 8, 1956, Robinson received the Spingarn Medal from the National Association for the Advancement of Colored People (NAACP). This prestigious medal is given annually to an African American outstanding in his or her field. Previous recipients include George Washington Carver, Justice Thurgood Marshall, and ironically, singer/actor Paul Robeson. Robinson was the first athlete awarded the medal. It meant that Robinson was the most admired African American of the time. It opened up many possibilities for life after baseball.

Then a few days after the medal presentation, Robinson received an offer to become vice president in charge of personnel for a company called Chock Full O'Nuts. Chock Full O'Nuts was a white-owned fast-food chain whose employees were mostly black.

Finally, on December 13, 1956, came shocking news. The Dodgers had traded Robinson to the team's longtime rivals—the New York Giants—for pitcher Dick Littlefield and $35,000. Robinson felt "surprised and stunned."[6] He was also in a bind. His contract with *Look* meant that he could not tell the Dodgers or the Giants that he was quitting to work for Chock Full O'Nuts. He had to stay silent until the issue telling of his retirement hit the newsstands. Finally the January 1957 *Look* was out. The world now knew that Jackie Robinson was quitting baseball.

Debate filled the sports pages. Some of the

Retiring after ten years as a major league player for the Brooklyn Dodgers, Robinson leaves the team clubhouse for the last time.

reporters who had covered Robinson's career were furious that he had not had an open news conference instead of selling his story to a magazine.[7]

The Giants offered to let Robinson name his own salary if he would change his mind and play for them. Robinson admitted that the generous offer, plus the pressure from fans to keep playing, gave him second thoughts.[8]

Then Buzzy Bavasi, general manager of the Dodgers, announced to the newspapers that Robinson was only saying he was going to work for Chock Full O'Nuts so that he could squeeze more money out of the Giants. Ever a man of principle, Robinson cast off any thought of staying in baseball—at least as a player. He might have considered a job as field manager or front-office executive, but those offers never came.

The way Robinson's career ended upset Hank Aaron, former Atlanta Brave and vice president of the Atlanta team, the first African American to hold this position in major league baseball. Robinson was someone special, who should always have had a place on the Dodgers, said Aaron. He should never have been traded.[9]

The man who teammate Roy Campanella said "could beat you every way there was to beat you . . . who was two steps and one thought ahead of anyone else," left baseball the same way that he had entered it—amid a fireball of controversy.[10]

11

NEW TRAILS
TO BLAZE

he state chapters of the NAACP named
February 16, 1958, Jackie Robinson Day. On
that day African Americans gathered in a
meeting hall in Jackson, Mississippi, to hear a speech
on civil rights. Outside, hostile whites surrounded the
hall. State and local police, expecting trouble, watched
and waited.

Around the country the civil rights movement was
heating up. Its goal was to end all forms of legal
segregation. In 1954 the Supreme Court, in *Brown v.
Board of Education*, declared school segregation illegal.

In 1955 African Americans, led by Martin Luther King, Jr., refused to ride buses in Montgomery, Alabama, until they could sit in any seat that they chose. A year later the Supreme Court upheld a lower court's decision that it was against the Constitution to have segregation on public transportation.

Still some southern states resisted any change. In September 1957 federal troops were needed to help launch integration at Central High School in Little Rock, Arkansas. A few days before Jackie Robinson Day, a Jackson Ku Klux Klan member had stated on the radio that his children would never go to school with black children. He said many white southerners would die to save their way of life with its Jim Crow laws.[1]

What better person to speak out against such bigotry than the man who had integrated baseball and proven that change was possible? The man now on stage at the Jackson hall was Jackie Robinson.

During the tense but peaceful meeting, Robinson reminded his listeners, inside the hall and out, that the Constitution was written for everyone. He urged them to use legal pressures to push for their rights, and not to stop until they had won them.[2]

Since he had retired from baseball fifteen months earlier, Robinson had become more focused on the fight for civil rights. He wanted to use his sports fame to open doors for groups fighting for equality. He also hoped to build bridges to the white establishment. Although his job with Chock Full O'Nuts was an important one—handling worker complaints, hiring and firing employees—his employer, William Black, gave him time off to pursue these personal goals.

Soon after his retirement the NAACP named Robinson chairperson of its 1957 Freedom Fund drive. The purpose of the drive was to raise funds through donations.

Requests for the new chairperson to appear poured in from all over the country. For the next year Robinson gave speeches nationwide. At first he spoke only a few minutes. As he became more familiar with the work of the NAACP and more comfortable as its speaker, his speeches stretched to a half hour. At the end of some talks he even raised money by selling kisses to the women. For the first time in its history, the yearly Freedom Fund drive earned over $1 million. His efforts earned Robinson election to the NAACP National Board of Directors in late 1957.

In 1958 and 1959 Robinson was at the height of his power as a voice for his people. He joined the "Youth March for Integrated Schools" in Washington, D.C. He had a weekly radio program. He wrote a column for the *New York Post*. In the column he commented on everything that interested him: politics, illegal drugs, youth violence, housing, education, and especially, civil rights. Robinson saw great potential in "the ballot and the buck"—using the power their votes and their money gave them to help African Americans gain their civil rights.[3]

Demonstrations, such as sit-ins, became common in the South in 1960. To call attention to businesses that did not treat blacks and whites equally, African Americans sat in the store or restaurant and refused to leave.

In Greensboro, North Carolina, four students were arrested during a sit-in. They did not ask Martin Luther King, Jr., for help, nor Roy Wilkins, the head of the NAACP. Instead, they asked Jackie Robinson. Robinson raised funds for the students by holding a concert on the lawn of his home in Stamford. Famous musicians such as Ella Fitzgerald, Duke Ellington, Sarah Vaughn, and Carmen McRae performed for free. This concert raised over $20,000.[4] It became a yearly event called the Afternoon of Jazz.

The year 1960 was also a presidential election year. Robinson turned his attention to politics. Robinson wanted a president dedicated to helping minority people. His first choice, Democrat Hubert Humphrey, lost his party's nomination to John F. Kennedy. Robinson then had to choose between the Democrat John F. Kennedy or the Republican Richard Nixon. Both Kennedy and Nixon wanted Robinson's support. Both thought that if Robinson supported one of them, other African Americans would too.

Robinson joins a picket line in 1960 to protest against restaurants
that refuse to serve African Americans. After his retirement from
baseball, Robinson continued to blaze a trail for civil rights.

Since the 1930s most African Americans had backed the Democratic party because the Republican party had a poor record on civil rights. Robinson believed that blacks needed to be active in both parties. He did not want the Republican party to include only whites. If baseball were integrated, but political parties were segregated, he said, it would make everything he worked for meaningless.[5]

Making a choice was difficult. To help him decide, he met the candidates. First Robinson met with Nixon. He thought that Nixon had a good record on civil rights and seemed eager to support the issues.

Robinson next met with Kennedy. The candidate admitted that he did not know much about the problems of African Americans, but was willing to learn. Robinson felt dismayed that a man running for President was so ignorant of their situation.[6] Kennedy also did not meet Robinson's gaze when they spoke. That upset Robinson.[7] He later wrote Kennedy a letter advising him to look people in the eye.

In September 1960 Robinson declared his support for Richard Nixon. He took a leave without pay from his job at Chock Full O'Nuts to help Nixon's campaign.

In October 1960 Martin Luther King, Jr., was jailed for picketing a store in Atlanta, Georgia. Robinson wanted Nixon to help King. Nixon remained silent. John F. Kennedy and his brother

Jackie Robinson backed Richard Nixon (shown shaking hands with Robinson) for President in 1960.

Robert, however, helped free the civil rights leader. Disappointed in Nixon, Robinson thought of quitting the campaign.[8] He later described backing Nixon as one of his poorer decisions.[9]

The following month Kennedy defeated Nixon for President. With the election over Robinson continued to work for civil rights. He had become well acquainted with Martin Luther King, Jr., and his organization, the Southern Christian Leadership Conference (SCLC). The NAACP did not like Robinson supporting the SCLC, which used nonviolent resistance to gain more rights. The NAACP preferred to use the law to gain rights.

Although he supported the goals of SCLC, even Robinson admitted that he would have had a hard time being a member. SCLC members stayed passive when attacked. Although he had done it once—to integrate baseball—Robinson did not think that he could do it again. Nevertheless he helped the SCLC whenever he could.

In 1961 Robinson helped King raise money to rebuild some Georgia churches burned by white racists. He also raised money for the SCLC's voter registration drive. This angered the leaders of the NAACP.[10]

Although Robinson still headed the Freedom Fund drive, he was becoming less active with the NAACP. He

Although he never became a member of King's Southern
Christian Leadership Conference, Jackie Robinson supported
Martin Luther King, Jr., by helping raise money for King's
organization and its causes.

thought that the leadership was too old, conservative, and timid to win the goals of integration.[11]

The next year, on January 23, 1962, an unusual incident happened. Jackie Robinson, now forty-three and his hair nearly snow-white, was speechless. To his surprise, baseball's sportswriters had voted him into the Baseball Hall of Fame.

To qualify for the Hall of Fame, a player must have been retired for five years and must have made a great contribution to the game. On that basis Robinson surely qualified. Yet because Robinson had such a stormy relationship with the press during his ten years of baseball, he had not expected to be approved. Now his election to the Hall of Fame meant that baseball fully accepted African Americans. Surprised and pleased, Robinson could think of nothing to say.[12]

On July 23, 1962, Robinson was inducted into the Baseball Hall of Fame in Cooperstown, New York. He asked three people to share the podium with him, people who were important to his career and his life: his mother, Mallie; his wife, Rachel; and his friend and mentor Branch Rickey.

The following year, in Birmingham, Alabama, King's SCLC was pushing for equal rights. Many demonstrations became violent. Police sprayed people with water hoses and threatened them with dogs. Someone bombed the motel where King was staying.

Robinson visited Birmingham in May 1963. With

When Robinson was inducted into the Baseball Hall of Fame on July 23, 1962, he asked his wife, Rachel, and his mother, Mallie Robinson, and Branch Rickey to share the podium with him.

King at his side he spoke at a local church. His voice shook. His words, full of emotion, inspired his listeners to continue the fight.

In September Robinson again returned to Birmingham. This time he visited a bombed church, where four little girls died. A friend remembered him standing there with "his fists shaking, trying to control his fury."[13]

Back home Robinson organized a rally to raise money to rebuild the church. Malcolm X, a young leader of the Nation of Islam, a militant black civil rights group, spoke first. More radical than King, Malcolm X was becoming a powerful influence in the drive for civil rights.

At the end of the rally Robinson thanked everyone for coming and said that they could go home. No one left. Instead the crowd started chanting for Malcolm X. Again Robinson told them to go. Again he was ignored. Some people began to get rowdy. At last Malcolm X reappeared and told everyone to leave. Obediently the crowd melted away.

Jackie Robinson had made the quest for equal rights possible. On that day the people benefitting from his trailblazing dismissed him in favor of a new hero, casting Robinson aside like yesterday's news.

12

THE END OF THE TRAIL

fter John F. Kennedy was assassinated in 1963, Lyndon B. Johnson became president. Jackie Robinson needed a new presidential candidate to champion in the 1964 election. He chose Nelson Rockefeller, then Republican governor of New York. In January 1964 Robinson quit his job with Chock Full O'Nuts to campaign for Rockefeller.

Robinson's support of Rockefeller disturbed Malcolm X. The two African-American spokesmen conducted a public debate in the newspapers. Malcolm X accused Robinson of letting himself be used by whites and of trying to "mislead" blacks into supporting Rockefeller, the way he had with Nixon. Robinson said that he did nothing to please anyone, black or white, unless it pleased *him*.[1]

Rockefeller lost the 1964 Republican nomination to Barry Goldwater. Robinson searched for a new project to occupy his time. Except for some old-timer games, he had not been a part of baseball for eight years. Now that he was out of the public eye, his views on politics and race did not get the attention that they once did. So turning his attention from "the ballot" to "the buck," he worked to create a new bank.

The Freedom National Bank opened in Harlem in December 1964. Owned mostly by blacks, it lent money to people usually turned down by white-owned banks.

Robinson was chairperson of the board. That position did not earn him a paycheck, however. He had not had a full-time job since leaving Chock Full O'Nuts. The few job prospects that appeared went nowhere. Fortunately Rachel had returned to school, had earned a degree in psychiatric nursing, and was helping support the family. Robinson admitted that he was upset about his wife going to work.[2]

Even more upsetting were Robinson's worries about his children. The Robinson children had been only nine, six, and four when their father left baseball. Now adolescents, they had done most of their growing

In 1964, Jackie Robinson campaigned for New York governor Nelson Rockefeller, who hoped to be the Republican party's choice for president. Rockefeller lost the nomination to Republican Barry Goldwater.

up after their father's work in the civil rights movement and in politics began keeping him away from home. Robinson realized that he had been so busy trying to propel other peoples' children toward a better life that he had neglected his own children.[3]

Jackie, Jr., had serious problems. He did not do well in school and had been labeled a troublemaker. Being the son of a famous person was difficult, and even more difficult if you shared the same name. Robinson admitted that he and his oldest son did not communicate well, even though they cared deeply about each other.[4]

Once, young Jackie ran away. Robinson searched his teenage son's room for clues to where he might be. He found a wallet with his own photo. Realizing that his son cared enough to carry his picture, Robinson broke down and cried. It was the only time, through all the good and bad years, that Rachel had seen him weep.[5] In 1964 seventeen-year-old Jackie joined the Army. Within a year he was in Vietnam.

Finally, in 1966, Rockefeller offered Robinson a job as his special assistant for community affairs. He was a go-between to both the black and white communities and stood in for the governor at special events. When it became clear that Nixon, not Rockefeller, would be the Republican's choice for President in 1968, Robinson left his job to campaign again for Democrat Hubert Humphrey, who lost to Nixon.

Robinson resigned from the board of the NAACP in 1967. He had not changed, Robinson claimed. The times had changed around him. When he first quit baseball, the conservative leaders of the NAACP found him too aggressive. Now, to the new militant groups, he was not aggressive enough.[6]

People began echoing Malcolm X's words—that Robinson's trail had been smoothed by white men, namely Branch Rickey, William Black of Chock Full O'Nuts, and Nelson Rockefeller. They remembered that Robinson, against the wishes of most African Americans, had supported Richard Nixon in 1960. Now they called Jackie Robinson an "Uncle Tom." An Uncle Tom is a black man who cooperates with whites to win their approval. This was a harsh name for the man who said, "I think, live, and breathe black first and foremost."[7]

The second half of the 1960s was a difficult time for Robinson. His friend Branch Rickey had died in 1965. In June 1967 Jackie, Jr., came home from Vietnam, wounded and addicted to drugs. For the next few months the young man drifted aimlessly. He broke into houses, stole, and sold drugs to support his habit.[8] In March 1968 he was arrested. He was carrying heroin, marijuana, and a .22-caliber pistol.[9]

At first Robinson wanted to disown his son. Then he threw his support behind him and listened to Jackie's story. It was a sad story of a young man bounced between the boredom and the terror of war. Jackie had tried to escape that boredom and that terror with drugs. Now he entered a drug rehabilitation program called Daytop.

In April 1968 Martin Luther King, Jr., was assassinated. That same year Robinson's mother, Mallie, died, and her son again had no job. When he left his position with Rockefeller, Robinson thought that the New York governor would offer him another after the election. No offer came. Two new businesses—a chain of seafood restaurants and a cosmetics store—did not succeed.

Robinson's health worsened. Only forty-nine, he had suffered two heart attacks, a minor one in 1962 and a more serious one in 1965. Diabetes had weakened blood vessels throughout his body. Now high blood pressure made them burst and bleed. Bleeding in the eyes caused his eyesight to fail. Bleeding in the legs made him lame.

Robinson started the 1970s with new hope. After two years in Daytop, Jackie, Jr., had begun to find his way. In the spring of 1971 he became a Daytop counselor, helping other drug-addicted young people. To aid the Daytop program he began planning an Afternoon of Jazz to be held at his parents' home. Jackie, Jr., and his father became closer than they had ever been. Then late on the evening of June 16, 1971, the young man's car spun out of control and crashed.

Twenty-four-year-old Jackie, Jr., died instantly. Robinson again wept for his son.

Six days after Jackie, Jr.'s, funeral, the Afternoon of Jazz occurred as planned. His father moved slowly from guest to guest, speaking quietly to each. Surrounded by music and by the people who had loved and helped his son, Robinson seemed to be at peace with his grief.

In the months that followed, Robinson worked with Alfred Duckett on a new autobiography titled *I Never Had It Made: An Autobiography*. It joined three other books that Robinson had written about his life. He also started the Jackie Robinson Construction Corporation, created to build low-cost homes.

In April 1972 Robinson attended the funeral of teammate Gil Hodges. Constant bleeding behind Robinson's eyes had blinded one eye and nearly destroyed vision in the other. He did not recognize his old friend Pee Wee Reese.

That June, twenty-five years after his first major league season, Robinson appeared at Dodger Stadium in Los Angeles. The Dodgers were retiring his number 42. A fan tossed a ball out of the stands for Robinson to autograph. It bounced off his head, because he could not see well enough to catch it. The state of Robinson's health shocked even his brother Mack.[10]

In October 1972 Robinson threw out the ceremonial ball at the second game of the World

Series. Then on national television he renewed his call for African Americans to move into baseball management. As usual criticism flew. Why did Robinson have to use the World Series to make such a request, newspaper reporters asked. "What better place?" Robinson replied. "What better time?"[11]

Only moments before, he had told former teammates Pee Wee Reese and Joe Black that he had to have his leg amputated. He had then assured the dismayed Reese that, once he mastered his artificial leg, he would still beat Reese at golf.[12]

Robinson never had the chance to make good on his boast. Nine days later, on October 24, 1972, fifty-three-year-old Jackie Robinson died of a heart attack at his home in Stamford. He had reached the end of the trail.

13

SAFE AT HOME

Millions mourned the death of Jackie Robinson. Famous people, including President Richard Nixon, wrote and spoke words of praise honoring the first African American to join modern major league baseball.

Hundreds of fans filed past Robinson's coffin at the Duncan Brothers Funeral Home. On October 27, 1972, over twenty-five hundred people filled New York's Riverside Church for his funeral service. These included politicians, sports figures, entertainers, and civil rights leaders. Most, however, were ordinary people—Jackie's fans. In them Jackie Robinson had instilled hope and pride.

A young minister named Jesse Jackson gave the main eulogy. Robinson was a black knight in a chess game, said Jackson, and he checkmated bigotry. The dates on his tombstone would read 1919–1972, Jackson continued, but it was on the dash between those dates that Robinson lived his life. "On that dash, he snapped the barbed wire of prejudice. . . . In his last dash, Jackie stole home and Jackie is safe."[1]

The funeral procession wound its way through the streets of the city—through Harlem, where it stopped before the Freedom National Bank; through Brooklyn, where Robinson had won the hearts of its citizens. Thousands lined the street to pay their final respects. Finally the cortege arrived at the Cypress Gardens Cemetery. There, Jackie Robinson was buried next to his son.

In 1986 President Ronald Reagan posthumously awarded Jackie Robinson the Presidential Medal of Freedom. This highest of civilian awards is given to a person who has made a great contribution to the nation. Robinson's widow, Rachel, accepted on her husband's behalf.

In 1990 *Life* magazine listed the century's most important Americans. Two baseball players made the list: Babe Ruth, who changed baseball, and Jackie Robinson, who changed baseball *and* America. He did this by battering down baseball's color barrier with dignity, determination, and talent. He also did it by making civil rights his passion long before protests, sit-ins, and marches came on the scene. Because of this, he is a more important figure in the fight for civil rights than history books acknowledge.

While calling for more recognition of Robinson in his hometown, Peter Dreier, a professor of politics in Pasadena, California, wrote, "His [Robinson's] efforts were as important as the Supreme Court's school desegregation decision or the Montgomery bus boycott in dismantling legal segregation and reducing bigotry."[2] Filmmaker Spike Lee would agree. He believes that "Jackie is one of the key figures in history in the 20th Century."[3]

Robinson would be pleased that, in April 1995, 40 percent of all major league baseball players were African Americans. Despite his pleas, however, there are few in executive or management jobs. In 1995 baseball boasted only one African-American vice president, one general manager, and one assistant general manager. Only three of the twenty-eight major league teams had African-American field managers.

". . . it is a sad commentary on Jackie Robinson's memory," wrote one newspaper reporter, "that 50 years later, the dirt he ate and the abuses he endured have had so little positive impact on management of the playing field."[4]

"How far have we come?" asked Tony Gwynn, African-American All-Star outfielder for the San Diego Padres. "Not very far at all. Will things get better in the future? Not really. Not until more people have the guts to step up and say, 'Here's a job.'"[5]

Jackie Robinson once wrote, "A life is not important except in the impact it has on other lives."[6] Robinson's life affected the lives of all Americans. That made his life very important indeed.

Ed Charles, former third baseman for the New York Mets, recalled a Dodgers' visit to his Florida hometown. After watching the rookie Robinson play a spring exhibition game, all the children ran after the train carrying the team. When they could run no farther, they put their ears to the tracks, listening as the train carried their hero toward his future. "We wanted to be part of him as long as we could," said Charles.[7]

Part of every young person belongs to Jackie Robinson. It is the part where secret dreams are stored. Jackie Robinson showed America's children, especially its African-American children, that these dreams do come true. In doing so, every child became a part of him forever—and he became a part of us all.

CHRONOLOGY

1919—Jack Roosevelt Robinson is born in Cairo, Georgia, on January 31.

1920—Robinson family moves to Pasadena, California.

1937—Enrolls at Pasadena Junior College.

1939—Enrolls at UCLA.

1942—Inducted into the United States Army.

1943—Commissioned as a second lieutenant.

1944—Court-martialed for insubordination; honorably discharged from the Army.

1945—Joins the Kansas City Monarchs of the Negro Baseball Leagues; meets with Branch Rickey and signs contract to play for Montreal Royals.

1946—Marries Rachel Isum; plays first game for Montreal Royals; son Jackie, Jr., is born.

1947—Plays first game for Brooklyn Dodgers; is named National League Rookie of the Year.

1949—Testifies before the House Un-American Activities Committee; wins National League's Most Valuable Player Award.

1950—Daughter Sharon is born; Robinson stars in the movie *The Jackie Robinson Story*.

1952—Son David is born.

1953—Integrates the dining room of the Netherlands-Plaza Hotel in Cincinnati and the Chase Hotel in St. Louis.

1955—Robinson family moves to Stamford, Connecticut; Brooklyn Dodgers win the World Series.

1956—Robinson receives the Spingarn Medal from the NAACP; traded to the New York Giants.

1957—*Look* magazine announces Robinson's retirement from baseball; becomes vice president of personnel for Chock Full O'Nuts; chairs the NAACP Freedom Fund drive.

1960—Campaigns for Richard Nixon for President.

1962—Inducted into the Baseball Hall of Fame.

1963—Visits Birmingham to support the fight for equal rights.

1964—Campaigns for Nelson Rockefeller for President; helps found the Freedom National Bank.

1966—Becomes special assistant for community affairs for Governor Rockefeller.

1968—Campaigns for Hubert Humphrey for President; Robinson's mother Mallie dies.

1971—Jackie Robinson, Jr., dies in a car accident.

1972—Robinson dies in Stamford, Connecticut, on October 24.

1986—Is posthumously awarded the Presidential Medal of Freedom.

1990—Is named by *Life* magazine one of the century's most important Americans.

CHAPTER NOTES

Chapter 1

1. Jackie Robinson as told to Alfred Duckett, *I Never Had It Made: An Autobiography* (Hopewell, N.J.: Ecco Press, 1995), p. 59.

2. Jules Tygiel, *Baseball's Great Experiment: Jackie Robinson and His Legacy* (New York: Vintage, 1984), p. 182.

3. Robinson and Duckett, p. 60.

4. Ibid., p. 60.

5. Ibid., p. 59.

6. Ibid., p. 61.

Chapter 2

1. Roger Kahn, *The Boys of Summer* (New York: Harper & Row, 1971), p. 391.

2. David Falkner, *Great Time Coming: The Life of Jackie Robinson, From Baseball to Birmingham* (New York: Simon & Schuster, 1995), p. 20.

3. Ibid., p. 33.

4. Jackie Robinson as told to Alfred Duckett, *I Never Had It Made: An Autobiography* (Hopewell, N.J.: Ecco Press, 1995), p. 266.

5. Maury Allen, *Jackie Robinson: A Life Remembered* (New York: Franklin Watts, 1987), p. 37.

Chapter 3

1. David Falkner, *Great Time Coming: The Life of Jackie Robinson, From Baseball to Birmingham* (New York: Simon & Schuster, 1995), p. 45.

2. Maury Allen, *Jackie Robinson: A Life Remembered* (New York: Franklin Watts, 1987), p. 27.

3. Falkner, p. 51.

4. Ibid., pp. 53–54.

5. Harvey Frommer, *Rickey and Robinson* (New York: Macmillan, 1982), p. 32.

Chapter 4

1. Jackie Robinson as told to Alfred Duckett, *I Never Had It Made: An Autobiography* (Hopewell, N.J.: Ecco Press, 1995), p. 12.

2. Donald Honig, *Baseball: When the Grass Was Real* (New York: Coward, McCann and Geoghegan, 1975), p. 310.

3. David Falkner, *Great Time Coming: The Life of Jackie Robinson, From Baseball to Birmingham* (New York: Simon & Schuster, 1995), p. 71.

4. Maury Allen, *Jackie Robinson: A Life Remembered* (New York: Franklin Watts, 1987), p. 27.

5. Jules Tygiel, *Baseball's Great Experiment: Jackie Robinson and His Legacy* (New York: Vintage, 1984), p. 63.

6. Robinson and Duckett, p. 23.

Chapter 5

1. Jackie Robinson as told to Alfred Duckett, *I Never Had It Made: An Autobiography* (Hopewell, N.J.: Ecco Press, 1995), p. 31.

2. Maury Allen, *Jackie Robinson: A Life Remembered* (New York: Franklin Watts, 1987), pp. 73–74.

3. Ibid., p. 75.

4. Robinson and Duckett, p. 31.

5. Ibid., p. 34.

6. Ibid., p. 34.

7. Jackie Robinson, *Baseball Has Done It* (New York: Lippincott, 1964), p. 43.

8. Jackie Robinson and Wendell Smith, *Jackie Robinson: My Own Story* (New York: Greenberg, 1948), p. 28.

9. Jules Tygiel, *Baseball's Great Experiment: Jackie Robinson and His Legacy* (New York: Vintage, 1984), p. 76.

10. Ibid., p. 75.

Chapter 6

1. Carl T. Rowan with Jackie Robinson, *Wait Till Next Year* (New York: Random House, 1960), p. 149.

2. Jackie Robinson as told to Alfred Duckett, *I Never Had It Made: An Autobiography* (Hopewell, N.J.: Ecco Press, 1995), p. 39.

3. Ibid., p. 40.

4. Ibid., p. 41.

5. David Falkner, *Great Time Coming: The Life of Jackie Robinson, From Baseball to Birmingham* (New York: Simon & Schuster, 1995), p. 128.

6. Rowan and Robinson, p. 144.

7. Ibid., p. 150.

8. Mark Harris, "Where've You Gone, Jackie Robinson?" *The Nation*, May 15, 1995, pp. 674–675.

9. Jules Tygiel, *Baseball's Great Experiment: Jackie Robinson and His Legacy* (New York: Vintage, 1984), p. 103.

10. Robinson and Duckett, p. 49.

11. Ibid., p. 50.

12. Ibid., p. 51.

13. Sam Maltin, "Fans Mob Jackie in Great Tribute," *Pittsburgh Courier*, October 12, 1946, p. 14.

14. Robinson and Duckett, p. 53.

Chapter 7

1. Carl T. Rowan with Jackie Robinson, *Wait Till Next Year* (New York: Random House, 1960), pp. 172–173.

2. David Falkner, *Great Time Coming: The Life of Jackie Robinson, From Baseball to Birmingham* (New York: Simon & Schuster, 1995), p. 152.

3. Geoffrey C. Ward and Ken Burns, *Baseball: an Illustrated History* (New York: Alfred A. Knopf, 1994), p. 291.

4. Jules Tygiel, *Baseball's Great Experiment: Jackie Robinson and His Legacy* (New York: Vintage, 1984), p. 188.

5. Falkner, p. 165.

6. Jackie Robinson as told to Alfred Duckett, *I Never Had It Made: An Autobiography* (Hopewell, N.J.: Ecco Press, 1995), p. 63.

7. Ibid., p. 63.

8. Maury Allen, *Jackie Robinson: A Life Remembered* (New York: Franklin Watts, 1987), pp. 127–128.

9. Falkner, p. 169.

10. Tygiel, p. 115.

11. Ibid., p. 196.

12. Roger Kahn, *The Boys of Summer* (New York: Harper & Row, 1971), p. 108.

13. Ibid., p. 108.

14. Falkner, p. 173.

15. Allen, p. 169.

16. Tygiel, p. 189.

17. Robinson and Duckett, p. 69.

18. Ibid., p. 69.

Chapter 8

1. Jackie Robinson as told to Alfred Duckett, *I Never Had It Made: An Autobiography* (Hopewell, N.J.: Ecco Press, 1995), p. 72.

2. Ibid., p. 73.

3. Ibid., p. 76.

4. Ibid., p. 75.

5. Ibid., p. 80.

6. Harvey Frommer, *Jackie Robinson* (New York: Franklin Watts, 1984), p. 66.

7. Robinson and Duckett, p. 80.

8. David Falkner, *Great Time Coming: The Life of Jackie Robinson, From Baseball to Birmingham* (New York: Simon & Schuster, 1995), p. 213.

9. Maury Allen, *Jackie Robinson: A Life Remembered* (New York: Franklin Watts, 1987), p. 170.

10. Jules Tygiel, *Baseball's Great Experiment: Jackie Robinson and His Legacy* (New York: Vintage, 1984), p. 326.

11. Robinson and Duckett, pp. 85–86.

12. Ibid., p. 86.

13. Harvey Frommer, *Rickey and Robinson* (New York: Macmillan, 1982), p. 166.

Chapter 9

1. Jules Tygiel, *Baseball's Great Experiment: Jackie Robinson and His Legacy* (New York: Vintage, 1984), p. 312.

2. Roger Kahn, *The Boys of Summer* (New York: Harper & Row, 1971), p. 105.

3. Maury Allen, *Jackie Robinson: A Life Remembered* (New York: Franklin Watts, 1987), p. 186.

4. Ibid., p. 180.

5. Tygiel, pp. 318–319.

Chapter 10

1. David Falkner, *Great Time Coming: The Life of Jackie Robinson, From Baseball to Birmingham* (New York: Simon & Schuster, 1995), p. 237.

2. Harvey Frommer, *Rickey and Robinson* (New York: Macmillan, 1982), p. 81.

3. Personal interview in May 1995 with St. Louis Cardinals fan, Jon Coombs, who was present for the elderly fan's comment.

4. Frommer, p. 163.

5. Ibid., p. 197.

6. Jackie Robinson as told to Alfred Duckett, *I Never Had It Made: An Autobiography* (Hopewell, N.J.: Ecco Press, 1995), p. 121.

7. Ibid., p. 122.

8. Ibid., p. 120.

9. Ibid., p. xvii.

10. Frommer, p. 204.

Chapter 11

1. David Falkner, *Great Time Coming: The Life of Jackie Robinson, From Baseball to Birmingham* (New York: Simon & Schuster, 1995), p. 268.

2. Ibid., p. 268.

3. Jackie Robinson as told to Alfred Duckett, *I Never Had It Made: An Autobiography* (Hopewell, N.J.: Ecco Press, 1995), p. 183.

4. Falkner, p. 274.

5. Roger Kahn, *The Boys of Summer* (New York: Harper & Row, 1971), p. 398.

6. Robinson and Duckett, p. 137.

7. Ibid., p. 137.

8. Ibid., p. 140.

9. Ibid., p. 135.

10. Falkner, p. 290.

11. Ibid., pp. 324–425.

12. Robinson and Duckett, p. 144, and Falkner, p. 290.
13. Falkner, p. 302.

Chapter 12

1. Jackie Robinson as told to Alfred Duckett, *I Never Had It Made: An Autobiography* (Hopewell, N.J.: Ecco Press, 1995), pp. 178–179.
2. Ibid., p. 159.
3. Ibid., p. 154.
4. Ibid., p. 154.
5. Ibid., p. 155.
6. Roger Kahn, *The Boys of Summer* (New York: Harper & Row, 1971), p. 406.
7. Robinson and Duckett, p. 18.
8. Ibid., p. 232.
9. David Falkner, *Great Time Coming: The Life of Jackie Robinson, From Baseball to Birmingham* (New York: Simon & Schuster, 1995), p. 326.
10. Harvey Frommer, *Rickey and Robinson* (New York: Macmillan, 1982), p. 224.
11. Ibid., p. 225.
12. Falkner, p. 342.

Chapter 13

1. Harvey Frommer, *Rickey and Robinson* (New York: Macmillan, 1982), pp. 226–227.
2. Peter Dreier, "In These Greedy Times, Remember Jackie Robinson," *Los Angeles Times*, March 22, 1995, p. B-7.
3. Kevin Baxter, "Hollywood Steps Up to the Plate," *Los Angeles Times*, June 18, 1995, p. 23.
4. Barry M. Bloom, "Since Jackie, Blacks Still Struggle For Equality," *San Diego Union-Tribune*, January 29, 1995, p. G-5.
5. Ibid., p. G-5.
6. Jackie Robinson as told to Alfred Duckett, *I Never Had It Made: An Autobiography* (Hopewell, N.J.: Ecco Press, 1995), p. 256.
7. Maury Allen, *Jackie Robinson: A Life Remembered* (New York: Franklin Watts, 1987), p. 4.

FURTHER READING

Books

Allen, Maury. *Jackie Robinson: A Life Remembered.* New York: Franklin Watts, 1987.

Falkner, David. *Great Time Coming: The Life of Jackie Robinson, From Baseball to Birmingham.* New York: Simon & Schuster, 1995.

Frommer, Harvey. *Rickey and Robinson.* New York: Franklin Watts, 1984.

Robinson, Jackie. *Baseball Has Done It.* New York: Lippincott, 1964.

———, and Alfred Duckett. *Breakthrough to the Big Leagues.* New York: Harper and Row, 1965.

———, as told to Alfred Duckett. *I Never Had It Made: An Autobiography.* Hopewell, N.J.: Ecco Press, 1995.

———, and Wendell Smith. *Jackie Robinson: My Own Story.* New York: Greenberg, 1948.

Rowan, Carl T., with Jackie Robinson. *Wait Till Next Year.* New York: Random House, 1960.

Scott, Richard. *Jackie Robinson.* New York: Chelsea House, 1987.

Tygiel, Jules. *Baseball's Great Experiment: Jackie Robinson and His Legacy.* New York: Vintage, 1984.

Ward, Geoffrey C., and Ken Burns. *Baseball.* New York: Knopf, 1994.

Video

Jackie Robinson. A & E Home Video, 1991.

INDEX